Delighting in God's Law is an excellent example of the interwoven connectivity of Scripture. By including insights into the law's historical context, Anyabwile unrolls the ancient scroll and unveils its beauty within. She walks with the reader, revealing the law's connection to the plan of redemption through Jesus.

AMY WILLIAMS
Managing Director of the Museum of the Bible and Archaeology and adjunct instructor for Thrive at New Orleans Baptist Theological Seminary

For those who find the Old Testament commands of God dry and boring, Kristie Anyabwile offers a refreshing deep dive into how the commands of God throughout Scripture invite us to know Him more and mirror His character in this world. She simply and applicably will help each reader grow in understanding God's Word as they study it and grow in delighting in the commands of God!

AMY GANNETT
Writer and Bible teacher, founder of The Bible Study Schoolhouse and Tiny Theologians

This book is just one reason why Kristie Anyabwile is one of my favorite Bible teachers today. I wish I had had this book the first few times I attempted to read through the Bible because it clarifies some of the most confusing biblical topics. Anyabwile's ability to use everyday illustrations to bring the metanarrative of Scripture to life is a gift from the Lord. The questions she asks are practical and helpful, and they will make a Bible scholar out of anyone who picks up this book.

LIV DOOLEY
Bible teacher; podcast host of *The Best Kept Secret*

This Bible study is a unique collection of teachings, questions, and details that would move any reader walking through it to grow in their faith, love for God's Word, evangelism, and biblical literacy. It also connects the Old and New Testament in profound ways that many may miss. And it gives the body of Christ a foundational framework for studying any chapter of the Bible.

PRICELIS PERREAUX-DOMINGUEZ
Author, *Being a Sanctuary*, Bible teacher, and founder of Full Collective

Delighting in God's Law is the study we need for a deep appreciation of the beauty of biblical law. We often read the law as intimidating or negative, but by the end of your time in Scripture (with Kristie as your guide) you will find yourself confident of its goodness.

PHYLICIA MASONHEIMER
Founder & CEO, Every Woman a Theologian

Kristie Anyabwile is a modern-day Ezra. After reading *Delighting in God's Law*, it was immediately clear to me that she is a disciple of Christ committed to studying, obeying, and teaching God's Word. In this study, she has provided both the novice and experienced Bible reader with a resource that will help them understand and respond to some of the most significant but challenging books of the Bible.

YANA JENAY CONNER
Discipleship Director, Vertical Church; author, *Through the Eyes of Color*

With much warmth and wisdom, Kristie Anyabwile has written a Bible study on God's law that is not only accessible but truly delightful to work through as the reader gains a greater understanding of the interplay between God's law and faith. She shows the reader how every promise of God finds its Yes in Jesus and that, in Him, God's commands are not a burden, but a delight. This study will give the reader fresh insight of what God's law is and why it matters for us today, too!

COURTNEY TRACY
Author, *Putting Jesus First: A 21-day Devotional Journey through Colossians*

For the average Christian, studying God's Old Testament Law can be a daunting challenge. However, Kristie has a gift for organizing and simplifying complex themes and offering the reader digestible truths so that God's law becomes accessible, relevant, and applicable to us today. *Delighting in God's Law* is theologically rich, inviting you to dive into your Bible as Kristie takes you on a journey through the law of God revealing the purpose of the law, God's plan for our lives, and ultimately how Christ is exalted.

SARITA T. LYONS
Director of Discipleship and Women's Ministry, Epiphany Church, Philadelphia; author, *Church Girl: A Gospel Vision to Encourage and Challenge Black Christian Women*

Kristie is a voice I trust. Her Bible teaching is solid, and her writing is brimming with delight for Jesus. Her Bible study, *Delighting in God's Law,* grounds you in the historical and cultural context of Scripture so that you can fully understand God's law as the life-giving, grace-filled path to Jesus. As soon as the word "law" is mentioned, I know Bible readers get skittish, but Kristie highlights that God's love came before the law. God's law doesn't restrain us; it shows us the way to Christ, who fulfills the law on our behalf.

KAT ARMSTRONG
Author, The Storyline Project Bible Studies; host, *Holy Curiosity* podcast

KRISTIE ANYABWILE

Delighting
in God's Law

OLD TESTAMENT
COMMANDS AND WHY
THEY MATTER TODAY

MOODY PUBLISHERS

CHICAGO

Edited by Pamela Joy Pugh
Interior and cover design: Kaylee Lockenour Dunn
Cover background of gold watercolor copyright © 2023 by Corca/Adobe Stock (250013549). All rights reserved.
Cover art of watercolor landscape copyright © 2023 by Marina/Adobe Stock (300319063). All rights reserved.
Author photo: Ayanna Shepherd

ISBN: 978-8024-2414-3

Originally delivered by fleets of horse-drawn wagons, the affordable paperbacks from D. L. Moody's publishing house resourced the church and served everyday people. Now, after more than 125 years of publishing and ministry, Moody Publishers' mission remains the same—even if our delivery systems have changed a bit. For more information on other books (and resources) created from a biblical perspective, go to www.moodypublishers.com or write to:

Moody Publishers
820 N. LaSalle Boulevard
Chicago, IL 60610

1 3 5 7 9 10 8 6 4 2

Printed in the United States of America

To Visha and Ruth,
without whom these
words would still be
in my head and heart
but not on the page.

CONTENTS

A Note for the Reader   *8*

    Summary of *Delighting*
    A Snapshot of Each Week
    Tips to Enhance Your Experience

Week One: Creation (Genesis 1)   *14*

Week Two: Covenant (Exodus 20)   *38*

Week Three: Consecration (Leviticus 20)   *64*

Week Four: Chaos (Numbers 14)   *94*

Week Five: Commitment (Deuteronomy 30)   *116*

Week Six: Christ in the Law   *140*

Conclusion   *171*

Outline of the Books of the Law   *174*

Acknowledgments   *175*

Notes   *176*

A NOTE FOR THE READER

It's Tuesday morning. You're sixty days into your Bible-in-a-year plan, and you have read almost four whole books of the Bible. What an accomplishment! A friend asks how your Bible reading is going and you try to piece together an answer. The stories in Genesis, Exodus, and Numbers were cool. Some of the stories seemed straightforward, but some, like today, with talking donkeys and weird dreams and confusing prophets had you scratching your head after the day's reading. From Leviticus, all you remember is a lot of blood and rules. As you decide how to respond to your friend, you realize you have more questions and few answers from what you've read so far.

If this has been your experience reading the Old Testament, you are not alone! It is intimidating. In addition to the complexity of each book, when we think of God's law, sometimes we are referring to the Ten Commandments. At other times we may think of lists of laws and rituals. And then there are even distinctions between moral, ceremonial, and civic law. How do we make sense of it all?

Here are some fundamental concepts to guide you as you begin your study of *Delighting in God's Law*. Let's start by understanding that the law encompasses all of God's commands, teachings, and instructions to His people. We see them most clearly in the first five books of the Bible, known as the *Pentateuch* (translated in Greek as "five books"). These five books—Genesis, Exodus, Leviticus, Numbers, and Deuteronomy—form the core of God's laws and instructions and serve as the foundation upon which the rest of the Bible unfolds. Because they catalog not just rules to obey but also instructions about life as a new, young nation, they are also called the *Torah*, from a Hebrew word that means "instruction." These books highlight a key biblical figure, Moses, who wrote down God's instructions and taught them to the people of Israel. Through Moses, God communicates with His people Israel, telling them who He is, who they are, and how and why He expects them to live in loving obedience to Him. Because of Moses' influence, these five books are also known as the *law of Moses*. Therefore, I will use *Torah, Pentateuch,* and *the law (or book of the law)* interchangeably throughout this study.

The law is the first grouping of books in the Bible that make up a *genre*, or category of biblical literature. Other genres found in the Old Testament are historical, poetic, narrative, wisdom literature, poetry, and prophecy. These genres are a cohesive unit, intentionally designed by God to tell His story.[1] Each book within the law articulates themes that help us to see its unique contribution to the genre, but these themes reverberate throughout the whole Bible, helping us to see the metanarrative of Scripture in a fresh way.

As one writer puts it, "The Torah initiates the story of redemption."[2] The story of redemption is that God creates, establishes, and sustains all life so that people would delight to bring Him glory by growing His kingdom and by growing in His likeness. The story takes a tragic turn at the very beginning when our first ancestors, Adam and Eve, sinned and strayed away from God's instructions. But God's plan continues to move forward and culminates in the death of God's Son, which reverses the curse brought upon the world by sin. The story ends with a new creation in a new heaven and new earth where God's people will perfectly love and glorify Him for eternity.

You will find *Delighting in God's Law* practical and valuable. You will uncover the context and purpose of God's commands, identify clues that reveal the theological significance of the law, and explore ways to appropriately apply the law to our lives today. You will discover that the law was not just for *those* people back *then*. It is for believers today. You don't have to be daunted by studying the law—you can be delighted by it!

SUMMARY OF *DELIGHTING*

Each book of the law has a unique purpose in helping us understand the significance of God's law as a whole. I have selected specific chapters from each book that encapsulate the purpose of the whole. This is intended to provide a helpful lens for understanding what God was communicating through that book about His plan of redemption that we see progressively revealed throughout Scripture.

CREATION . . . . Genesis 1

COVENANT . . . . Exodus 20

CONSECRATION . . . . Leviticus 20

CHAOS . . . . Numbers 14

COMMITMENT . . . . Deuteronomy 30

CHRIST IN THE LAW . . . . Galatians 3

As we work through this study using the selected passages above, we will see that God *created* humanity to be in a *covenant* relationship with Him. He calls us to *consecrate* our lives to Him in holiness. Though humanity would rebel in *chaos* against His instructions, God kindly continues to call His people to fully *commit* our lives to Him in obedience so that we might receive the blessings that come through our relationship with *Christ*. Jesus was present in creation. He kept all of God's commands perfectly. He helps us be consecrated to God in holiness. Jesus is victorious over the chaos of sin in the world and in our hearts. Christ has committed Himself to save all all who repent of their sins and trust in Him. This study is centered on the One who gave us His law and the One who fulfills it.

DEFINITIONS

COVENANT: A special commitment between God and His people that God initiates, maintains, and fulfills. God's covenant requires obedience and promises blessing for the people of God.

CONSECRATION: Full devotion to God in holiness and by living completely distinct from those who don't know and love God.

A SNAPSHOT OF EACH WEEK

Each week will highlight a way in which God unfolds the purposes of His law for the people of Israel and for us, including five days of study that follows the following plan:

DAY ONE: Context of the passage. This first day will focus on background information related to our specific passage. Since each passage is a small snippet of the book that it falls within, we will need to know what occurred before and after the passage under discussion, specifically as it relates to God's law.

DAY TWO: Command of the text. On this day, we work verse by verse through the chapter to discover what the text is commanding its original audience to know, understand, think, do, believe, or act on.

DAY THREE: Clues about Christ and other parts of Scripture. All of Scripture relates to Jesus' life, death, and resurrection in some specific and meaningful way. Our goal is to see how our passage looks forward to or speaks about Jesus. We also want to see ways in which our passage connects to broader biblical themes and the New Testament.

DAY FOUR: Carry the text with you. We aim to accurately apply the text to our lives now, considering what God expects from His people today. We will explore ways in which we exercise, fall short of, and activate our faith in Christ to help us live more closely aligned with His heart for us.

DAY FIVE: Contribution to the law. Finally, we close our week with a look at how our passage helps us see the overall theme of the book and its unique contribution to the law genre.

QUESTIONS FOR GROUP REFLECTION

You might find it helpful to go through this study with others, so questions for group reflection are offered at the end of each week. But even if you're going through *Delighting* on your own, these closing-week questions will help you summarize what you have learned and incorporate these insights into your life and in further study of God's Word.

TIPS TO ENHANCE YOUR EXPERIENCE

I consider Bible study unique among the available Bible literacy options. In all the ways that we connect with God's Word, we are reliant on God's Spirit to teach and guide us. For example, with a devotional method, the study, interpretation, application, and often a prayer prompt is already done for you, which is great at times! When your time is short, and you just need an encouraging word to carry you through the day, this is a very helpful way to take in God's Word.

However, in Bible study, *you* do the hard and rewarding work of study, interpretation, application, and prayerful response on your own. This takes time. You need plenty of time for not only reading, but for writing down questions, chasing down answers, meditating on the truth of God's Word, and living in light of what you learn.

Bible study is a holistic discipline that engages the heart and the mind of the student but also each person of the Trinity. God illuminates His Word to us, and the effort we put forth is out of the strength that Christ supplies (Col. 1:29). The Holy Spirit is our teacher and guides us into all truth. We need all of us and all of God in our study. With that in mind, here are a few tips to guide you into getting the most from *Delighting*:

- **PRAY** before, during, and after your study. Ask God for *understanding,* ask Jesus for strength, and ask the Holy Spirit for guidance.

- **READ** in different Bible *translations* (e.g., ESV, CSB, NIV, NLT).

- **LISTEN** to the Bible on *audio.*

- **OBSERVE** the type of *text* you are studying. Is it a story, or a speech, or a poem, or laws?

- **EXAMINE** the *context* of the passage. Context can be:

    literary, referring to the text that surrounds the passage we are studying,

    historical, what was happening in history at the time this passage was written,

    cultural, the circumstances of the original audience, or

    biblical, when the author uses familiar biblical references to cue the audience.

- **LOOK** for *repetitions* of words and phrases.

- **FOLLOW** *transition words.* Transition words help us move through a passage by connecting ideas.

    And: adds to an idea

    By, because: why or how something is done

    So that, therefore, thus: concluding

    But, however: contrasting

    After that, now, then: time references

- **CONSIDER** what the passage would have meant to the *original audience.*

- **RELY** on the *Holy Spirit* for guidance, remembering that as we do our part, the Holy Spirit will open the eyes of our heart (Eph. 1:17–18).

Creation

(GENESIS 1)

[Abraham] believed the Lord, *and he*
counted it to him as righteousness. *—Genesis 15:6*

*E*veryone likes a good origin story. The Marvel comic book series and movie franchise introduced us to the origin of the infinity stones. We learned that before the Marvel universe began, six singularities controlled various aspects of existence.

According to this fiction series, after the big bang, these singularities were somehow compressed into stones and scattered throughout the universe. Those who possessed a stone could control a specific aspect of reality, such as mind, space or time control, teleportation, power and energy manipulation, and altering reality. Glimpses of these stones in the various Marvel movies only allows us partial understanding of their power. But when we trace the origin, we get a fuller picture of how each character who possesses a stone reflects the origin, why Thanos is so morbidly intent on collecting all of them, and why it is critical to keep them from him.

We also learn that the original intent of the stones was to govern the universe and that they were not meant for the whims of fallen (though powerful) mortal beings. Even those who wielded a stone somewhat righteously ended up dying because of it.

Genesis 1 is an origin story, not one that starts with a big bang that throws the universe into chaos, but it starts with the God of the universe who, in love, created the world and everything in it. By the power of His Word, He ushers forth life and order and meaning. And with that same power He offers to redeem and bless humanity through an unlikely offspring.

As you complete this week's study, ask the Lord to help you delight in the law by understanding His power, His work, and His blessings to humanity through the creation story.

DAY ONE

CONTEXT OF THE PASSAGE

Before the creation of the world, there were no multiple singularities. God was and is the singular Being who has always existed. He did not need anyone or anything (Acts 17:25). Yet, it was God Himself who planned from before the foundation of the world to create and to redeem a people for Himself (Eph. 1:4). But why? The Bible teaches us that God created both the heavens (Ps. 19:1) and humanity for His glory (Isa. 43:7). God's glory has to do with His greatness, with the honor He deserves as sovereign ruler of all things. It is often referred to as His "weightiness." His glory is the ultimate purpose of all creation.

This study begins by meditating on the untainted beauty, grandeur, and perfection of God's place and people under His presence, as a display of His glory.

Every passage of the Bible is influenced by the verses surrounding it. We call this the literary context. But Genesis 1 starts the whole Bible! So what would be the literary context? While we cannot point to a passage that exists before Genesis 1, we do know that Scripture has a lot to say about what happened "before the beginning" of the world. We can look both inside and outside Genesis 1 at the larger biblical context to learn more about the work and mind of God in creation. When you read the whole of the book of Genesis, you will see the power of God and the weakness of humanity on display. As we unpack the beginning of human history, keep in mind that Genesis was written for the first generation of Israelites during their desert wanderings. They had been freed from slavery in Egypt and were looking forward to entering the land that God had promised them. As a people without a home, traveling through a region that was full of false gods, the Israelites were vulnerable to the people and cultures around them. The book of Genesis reminds these wandering God-followers to persevere in obedience, trusting in God's power to protect and keep them, His work in guiding and providing for them, and His promise to bless them in the land that He had given. Let's dive into this week looking for God's power, work, and blessings on display from the beginning.

READ GENESIS 1:1–2.

What stands out to you as you read? Throughout this study, you are encouraged to circle or underline phrases that are repeated and highlight what seems significant to you. It's okay to write in your Bible!

What aspects of God's character do you see most clearly in this passage?

Read these passages and write down what was going on before "the beginning" or "before the foundation of the world."

PASSAGE	NOTES
JOHN 17:5, 24	
PSALM 90:1–2	
PROVERBS 8:22–31	
REVELATION 13:8	
EPHESIANS 1:4	
ACTS 17:24–27	
1 PETER 1:19–21	

In a sentence, what are these passages communicating about what happened "before the foundation of the world"?

Read these passages and write down what you learn about the work of God in creation and the mind of God in creation. What words describe the activity of God in creation? How or why did He create these things?

PASSAGE	GOD'S WORK IN CREATION	HOW OR WHY GOD CREATED IT
EXAMPLE: PSALM 33:6	HEAVENS MADE BY GOD'S WORD; THE HEAVENLY HOST BY HIS BREATH	BY HIS WORD BY HIS BREATH
JOB 38:4–7		
PSALM 136:5		
ISAIAH 40:12–14, 18–22, 25–26		
ISAIAH 45:18		
ACTS 17:24–27		
COLOSSIANS 1:16–17		
HEBREWS 11:3		
REVELATION 4:11		

What do you learn about God from this exercise that echoes what you wrote earlier?

What truths from Genesis 1:1–2:3 would sustain Israel as they wandered?

How might these same truths sustain you?

DAY TWO

COMMAND OF THE TEXT

Many people struggle at the beginning of their Bible study time, unsure if they really understand what a passage means. One reason for this struggle is that we often look for the *why* before we have really explored the *what*. In other words, we try to discover meaning and application before we get the basic message that the Scripture writer was communicating to his audience.

For this reason, I have found it helpful to read very slowly so that I can ask lots of questions about the words in and around my passage: the people, places, things, and word pictures in the passage, as well as the situation in which the passage was written. Sometimes the author is taking the reader on a journey where there is a question posed and answered, or a problem presented and solved, or a conflict developed and resolved. Sometimes they want to remind them about who God is and what He has done and is doing in their lives. Sometimes they want the reader to see the logical conclusion resulting from a set of beliefs, actions, or thought patterns.

This process of slow reading and asking plenty of questions helps me make what I hope are "obvious observations." Through these obvious observations, I'm prayerfully asking the Lord to allow the Word to take on shape and structure and order, to help me see—as the elder saints used to say, "what thus saith the Lord"— so that I can grasp *what* God, through the biblical author, is saying to those who would have first heard or read the passage.

If Scripture seems unclear, we need a process for seeing what is plainly there. It's sort of like driving through fog. Even if you've been on the same road or highway before, fog makes you question every acceleration and every turn. Dense fog can make you hover over your brakes, nervous to take your foot off and give the car a little gas, lest you run into something unforeseen and damage your car.

But as the fog clears, the questions that once induced fear and doubt give way to discovery and beauty. Instead of the dreaded, "Oh no! I have no idea what's ahead and I'm afraid to move forward," the thought becomes, "Oh wow! I'd never noticed that landmark before or those flowers."

Clearing away the fog doesn't negate questions but embraces them as opportunities for revealing insights that were previously obscured by the fog of uncertainty and whatever else keeps us from clearly seeing what is there. The beauty of slow reading and careful observation is that it leads to discovering God's revealed truth in the Bible. It also demonstrates that God is extraordinarily intentional about every word of His God-breathed, Spirit-illuminated, Christ-centered Word. Once we learn *what* a passage is about, then we can move on to asking *why* the writer says what they say, what it would have meant to the original biblical audience, and how it relates to our lives today.

I have listed some questions below that will help you to make some obvious observations about the text, meaning the answers to the questions come directly from the passage and help you see the overall arrangement of the passage. There are also questions that will guide you to derive meaning from the verses, that encourage you to understand what God intends to teach you about Himself and about humanity.

The Israelites would have to go back to "the beginning" and remember who their God is and why He created them. So now let's consider what these opening verses in Genesis command us to understand and believe about God in creation.

Who is the subject in these verses? What did He do and when? What does this teach us about Him?

What phrases are repeated, and why did the writer use repetition?

.

List all the things that God created. What does this teach us about Him?

READ GENESIS 1:26–31.

What transition words are new to this section? Remember, transition words are *and*, *but*, *then*, and so on.

What is unique about this aspect of God's creation in verses 26–27?

In verses 28–31?

What does this teach us about God's plan for humanity? Use words from the text.

READ GENESIS 2:1–3.

What verbs stand out in these verses and why?

Based on your answers to the questions above, think of a title for each of these sections. These titles will serve as an outline that helps us see how the author has organized the passage:

Genesis 1:1–2

Genesis 1:3–25

Genesis 1:26–31

Genesis 2:1–3

Putting it all together, write a sentence (or two) that communicates what Genesis 1–2:3 would have meant to the Israelites.

The opening chapter of Genesis was written in the context of a people who are surrounded by competing lesser gods and who feel the limits of their abilities. This passage reminds Israel that God created all things as a demonstration of His limitless nature and unrivaled power, to bless His creation. As we move through the book of Genesis, we see that the blessing of God is quickly challenged by Satan, but God's plan was never meant to be fulfilled through Adam in the garden.

DAY THREE

CLUES ABOUT CHRIST

God existed when there was nothing. By the power of His Word, He went to work, showcasing His glory through the creation of the world with order, mystery, creativity, and specificity. Indeed, the heavens and earth declare and proclaim His glory and His work. God created people to reflect His glory, to represent Him in the world, and to rule over all the things He created.

Upon hearing this recounting of the creation, maybe the wandering Israelites would trust that God had not forgotten them. Maybe they would look for ways in which God showcased His glory in their wilderness wandering. Maybe they would see how God continued to bless them as a growing nation, providing food, clothing, leadership, protection.

Maybe they would be encouraged to keep walking in faith in the wilderness, in anticipation of His glory being revealed in a way they did not expect. No human could perfectly reflect God's glory, perfectly represent Him, perfectly rule over His creation, perfectly keep His instructions and commands. God's glory would be revealed, and amazingly, God chose to *share* His glory with us (John 17:22–24)! God would indeed bless humanity ultimately through Christ. Let's explore ways in which Genesis 1 gets us to Jesus.

From the passages below, what do you learn about Christ's power, work, and how He blesses humanity?

JOHN 1:1–16

What is the interplay between the power of God and the work of God?

How was the work of God meant to bless humanity?

ROMANS 1:18–20

What aspect of God's power do we learn about and how does God display His power?

What do we learn about God's "eternal power and divine nature" (v. 20)?

What do verses 16–17 say about Christ's power and work?

What else do we learn about the work of Christ in verses 18–20?

From verse 20, how does Christ bless humanity?

HEBREWS 1:1–4

What are the actions of God mentioned in these verses?

What do these verses say about the power of God?

How do the works of God bless humanity?

Write a sentence that communicates what you learn about Christ from Genesis 1.

Close your time today in prayer, delighting in God for blessing humanity through the gospel of His Son.

DAY FOUR

CARRY THE TEXT WITH YOU

Many of us have been taught that to have a fruitful time in the Word, we must conclude our devotions with personal application. We must ask the question, "What does it mean to me?" While this is not a bad practice per se, it would be easy for us to mistakenly think that God's Word is *about* us and *for* us. However, the Word of God is about *God* and for us. It's not necessary to look for ways to personally apply every single passage, though we will do a lot of that in this study. Reading Scripture for the sake of communing with the Lord, seeing facets of His character come alive, is a wonderful way to carry God's Word with us throughout our day.

However, there are truths from every passage of Scripture, and specifically this week, from the creation account, that are essential for us to understand about God and about ourselves. We need to know who God is, who we are as created beings, and what God expects from us. Today we'll examine ways to apply what we're learning about God and His creation to our daily life.

What do we need to remember from Genesis 1–2:3, and how do we respond to the truth of this portion of Scripture?

Christ created all things, He rules all things, and we are subject to Him
(Ps. 24:1–2; John 1:1). Take a moment to acknowledge Christ's work in your life.
Then reflect on the following:

How can you demonstrate that you believe Christ is worthy of your trust?

In what areas of your life do you find it difficult to acknowledge that "Christ did that" (e.g., friendships, finances, health, leisure)?

How can you grow in submitting more areas of your life to Him?

Christ demonstrated His limitless nature and unrivaled power through His life, death, and resurrection. Our proper response is to submit to Christ's power in our life.

What things rival for power in your life over Christ? Consider rival belief systems, rival identities, even natural occurrences.

How can you see Christ's divine power at work in your life?

CHRIST'S BLESSING

Christ desires to bless humanity through the gospel. Our proper response is to receive His blessing by believing the gospel and trusting in Christ for salvation. When we receive Christ's blessing of salvation, we should seek to bless others.

What can you do to:

multiply disciples?

fill the earth with the knowledge of God?

call people to submission to Him?

steward God's creation well?

Reflect on Christ's saving grace and express your gratitude to Him in a prayer.

DAY FIVE

CONTRIBUTION TO THE LAW

Genesis 1 is the beginning of the Book of Beginnings. In it, we see so much of God. We've talked a lot about His power, work, and blessings, and connected those things to Christ. But let's see how these themes also echo throughout the book of Genesis to give us a clearer picture of how this first chapter ties into the rest of the book.

When we are studying any book of the law, we want to read it in light of the whole. The commands, rules, instructions, blessings, and consequences that we see throughout the book of Genesis must all be viewed in light of who God is and what He is up to.

There are many other themes that we could trace through the book of Genesis that are echoed throughout Scripture, but let's keep working on the themes that we have discovered so far.

As you read these passages from Genesis, you will likely see a lot of overlap. This is great because it indicates the unity of the Scriptures, and how interrelated God's power, work, and blessing are in accomplishing His purposes.

What do you learn about the work of God in creation?

What do you learn about God's power?

What do you learn about how God would bless His people?

Noah (Gen. 9:8–17)

Abram (Abraham) (Gen. 12:1–3)

Isaac (Gen. 26:1–5)

Jacob (Gen. 35:9–13)

How do these themes contribute to your understanding of God's law?

Literarily, although Genesis is primarily narrative, it serves the purpose of helping us see the whole of Genesis as a book about our Creator God in all His power, wisdom, and majesty, choosing before the foundation of the world to create a people He would bless and multiply through a special offspring who would come through the family of Abraham. This offspring would crush the head of the serpent, destroying the works of the devil (Gen. 3:15).

In the sacrifice of Abraham's "one and only son" Isaac, the offspring through whom all the nations would be blessed is Christ (Gal. 3:16) and therefore all people whose faith is in Jesus are Abraham's children (Gal. 3:7) and partakers of the blessings that God promised in Genesis. What undergirds the law is the idea that God's blessings come through the gospel. We should delight in *Jesus*, who created all things as a demonstration of His limitless nature and unrivaled power, to bless humanity through His gospel.

Now that we've laid the foundation of God's creative work, next week we'll look at the covenant He made with His people.

QUESTIONS FOR GROUP REFLECTION

1. How does creation set the stage for the unfolding of God's redemptive plan through Christ?

2. How does our responsibility to care for creation reflect our gratitude for the blessings we receive through the gospel?

3. How does gratitude for God's blessings expressed through creation lead us to a deeper worship of Him?

4. How does Christ's role in creation inform our witness to others?

Covenant

(EXODUS 20)

*And when I see the blood, I will pass over you,
and no plague will befall you to destroy you,
when I strike the land of Egypt. —Exodus 12:13*

I grew up listening to iconic music artists such as Whitney Houston, Prince, Madonna, New Edition, Michael Jackson, Run-DMC, MC Lyte, Salt-N-Pepa, and oh so many others! Music from the eighties is made for dancing. I get in most of my cardio by dancing in-between sets of presses and squats. However, sometimes a song will come through my playlist that's outside the norm. Sometimes the lyrics of a song "hit different."

This happened recently with a song that I remembered from my childhood. The song opens with the artist saying he trusted and loved someone who led him along but who never kept their promises. The refrain repeated the idea that someone made promises to them that they neither believed nor intended to keep. You can almost feel the weight of betrayal and lies and wordsmithing from someone who will lie and say just about anything to get what they want.

I wonder if this is how Israel felt as they waited on the promises of God to come to pass. Would the God whom they trusted and loved keep His promises? Was God sending this people on a road to nowhere? The answer of course is no. God is not sending them on a cosmic goose chase. Unlike the song, God always keeps His promises. He cannot lie. He will do all that He promises.

We saw in the last day of Week One that God made promises to Abraham, to Isaac, and to Jacob. We call these men the "patriarchs" because they are the fathers whose family line God promised to bless with children who would form a massive nation. He promised that through this nation, Israel, all nations would receive God's blessing. He promised land where Israel would live under His blessing and rule. That promise seemed more likely at some points in their early history than others, but by the close of Genesis, the Hebrew people were thriving, and they were waiting for God to provide the land of promise. Meanwhile, they were living in Egypt. Jacob's son Joseph, after some considerable difficulties (see Gen. 37–50), had risen to be a high-ranking official in Egypt. He eventually brought his family to live there. If you're not familiar with the story of Joseph—and how he and his extended family got to Egypt—I recommend you read the biblical account found in Genesis 37–50. It sounds like a lot of reading, but I assure you that it is an action-packed and fast-paced true story of God's actions among His people.

As you complete this week's study, pray that the Lord will help you delight in the law by seeing how His promises can be trusted through the enactment of His covenant with His people.

DAY ONE

CONTEXT OF THE PASSAGE

EXODUS 20

When the book of Exodus opens, it's over four hundred years after Joseph and his brothers had settled in Egypt. The Israelites have grown in number and in strength, so much so that the pharaoh of Egypt felt threatened by them and forced them into slavery. The Hebrew people cried out to the Lord for help, and the Lord raised up Moses as their leader, speaking to him from a burning bush. You may be familiar with this account told in Exodus 3.

The Lord responded to the groanings of Israel, saying, "I observed you and what has been done to you in Egypt, and I promise that I will bring you up out of the affliction of Egypt to the land of the Canaanites . . . a land flowing with milk and honey" (Ex. 3:16b–17). It took some doing, like ten plagues' worth of doing, because of the hard-heartedness of the Egyptian pharaoh.

The last plague was one of darkness and death throughout Egypt of every firstborn human and animal. Pharaoh's obstinance finally ran out, and in the middle of the night, he released Israel from their servitude, and over 600,000 men, along with women and children and even their livestock, left Egypt. There was a solemn assembly to observe a special Passover meal to commemorate God passing over the people of Israel and protecting them from the dreadful firstborn plague. There was also a special feast of unleavened bread and consecration of the firstborn children that would be an annual reminder for Israel of what God had done for them in delivering them from slavery in Egypt and protecting their firstborn children.

It was also at this time that God began to direct the travels of Israel with a cloud during the day and a pillar of fire by night. God showed up for them in a big way. Not only did He demonstrate His power before them in the plagues, but He also used Moses to push back the waters of the Red Sea so Israel could cross it safely—on dry land!—because of course Pharaoh couldn't leave well enough alone. The impact of losing hundreds of thousands of enslaved people in one go would make any heartless ruler think twice. So Pharaoh showed up and God showed out.

When all the people of Israel had safely crossed the sea, the Lord released the water back in its place, drowning all of Pharaoh's militia who had attempted to follow Israel across the sea. Of course, the people celebrated; they feared the Lord because of His power, and they believed in God and in His servant Moses, at least for the time being.

Only three days into their journey in the wilderness outside Egypt, the people grumbled about the water. Sure, it was bitter, but with all the miraculous displays of power they had seen God perform, you would think their trust-ometer would be a bit higher. Not so. Two weeks later, they complained about not having enough food and God abundantly supplied them with manna and quail. God continued to respond to their grumbling with provision and protection.

As we begin this week's study, we start our journey of understanding God's covenant with Israel. A covenant is an agreement or treaty between two parties, but as you study the Ten Commandments this week and the response of Israel to them, you will see that these commandments are not merely rules. They are meant by God to reveal Himself to Israel, to call them into a special relationship with Him, so that they might respond in proper worship of God.

Chapter 19 establishes the context of when and where God gives Israel the Ten Commandments.

According to verses 1–2, where are the Israelites?

According to verses 3–6, what does God call Israel to do? Who is God calling them to be?

How does Israel respond to the Lord? See verses 7–8.

What is your response to the Lord? Meditate on that as we close this day.

What stands out to you as you read?

What aspects of God's character do you see most clearly in this passage?

DAY TWO

COMMAND OF THE TEXT

Bible scholars place the Ten Commandments in the category of ancient treaties. In particular, a suzerain treaty is a covenant or treaty between two parties involving a suzerain—a ruler or person of authority—who comes into agreement with subjects under their rule. They were common often among kingdoms whose goal was to set rules and terms for governance and order. The suzerain would introduce himself as the one in authority and the subjects would recognize his right to rule and pledge their allegiance.

The terms and conditions of the treaty would be carefully outlined, including the length of the treaty and consequences for violation. Although there are elements of this kind of treaty with the Ten Commandments, God is not an earthly ruler. He is the divine King of the universe. His commands are not political, but moral and ethical instructions that call His people into a loving relationship with Him and with one another. As His people, we enter into this covenant as worshipers of the true and living God who love Him and desire to please Him from the heart.

How does God identify Himself? What did He do for Israel? How do you think this would have impacted their posture toward God (how they would have listened to the Ten Commandments)?

Summarize each commandment in your own words.

1st

2nd

3rd

4th

What relationship do those commandments speak to?

READ EXODUS 20:12–17.

Summarize each commandment in your own words.

5th

6th

7th

8th

9th

10th

What relationship do those commandments speak to?

Use these cues to describe the scene in these four verses: **What did the people see? In your answer, include their emotional, physical, and verbal responses. What did they ask Moses to do?**

What physical, verbal, and (implied) emotional response did Moses demonstrate?

READ EXODUS 20:22–26 AND JOT DOWN ANSWERS TO THESE:

Which commandments does God repeat? What are God's instructions to Israel? Why does God give these instructions?

What are some areas of emphasis in Exodus 20?

From the previous question, you may have found a few areas of emphasis. Let's quickly recap by considering the basis on which God initiated His relationship with Israel (vv. 1–2), the relationships that were emphasized in the Ten Commandments (vv. 3–11 and 12–17), the Israelites' response (vv. 18–21), and how God expected them to respond to His law (vv. 22–26).

Putting it all together, write a sentence that communicates what Exodus 20 would have meant to the Israelites.

DAY THREE

CLUES ABOUT CHRIST

God reveals Himself personally to Israel, giving them commands that highlight both the vertical relationship of God to His people and the horizontal relationship of the people toward one another.

God tells them in Exodus 20:6 that His goal is to show His steadfast love to those who love Him and keep His commandments. This changes dramatically how some understand the Ten Commandments. They are not demands from a harsh ruler. They establish the kind of loving relationship that God wants with His people and the kind of loving relationship that He wants His people to have in covenant community. Jesus quotes Deuteronomy 6:4–5 in His response to the lawyer who asked Him which was the greatest commandment. Jesus said, "You shall love the Lord your God with all your heart and with all your soul and with all your mind. This is the great and first commandment. And a second is like it: You shall love your neighbor as yourself. On these two commandments depend all the Law and the Prophets" (Matt. 22:37–40).

Of course, Israel was never able to obey as God had commanded. Moses was still on the mountain when they made the golden calf (Ex. 32:1–6). Their history was marked by continual violation of God's moral law. Loving God and neighbor perfectly was never within the capabilities of Israel nor us. We see why Israel may have been so afraid (Ex. 20:18)—they stood far off because they knew that they could not stand before a holy God.

So, they pleaded with Moses to serve as their mediator. A mediator is sort of a middle person who stands in the gap between two parties, in this case between God and Israel. As mediator, Moses had the privilege to speak to the people on God's behalf, and to speak to God on behalf of the people. Moses helped to bridge the relational gap between God and His people. Let's take a closer look at what the New Testament teaches us about how believers today can come into a relationship with God and respond to Him rightly.

How do believers come into a right relationship with God according to Romans 5:19?

According to Philippians 2:8, what was the extent of Christ's obedience?

READ 1 TIMOTHY 2:5-6A AND HEBREWS 9:15.

If Moses was the mediator for Israel, who is the mediator for believers today? How is this new mediator's work accomplished?

According to Romans 8:1–4, what are those in Christ free from?

How do we obtain that freedom?

How is the righteous requirement of the law now fulfilled?

How is Jesus as our mediator better than Moses as a mediator for Israel?

How should believers respond to Christ as our mediator?

In Exodus 20, God sets forth His commands that Israel was expected to obey. The first two commands concern God as the Divine Being whom they should worship rightly by putting Him first, above all else. God's directive to the people of Israel is like this: "I have purposed to be in covenant relationship with you and I want you, in like manner, to live in covenant community with each other as you worship Me in reverential fear."

The people heard all the commands of God and they saw His power on display on the mountain, and they immediately realized they were in trouble. What God required was impossible for them and they knew it. They couldn't come before a holy God who had delivered them from the hand of Pharaoh, who expected to be worshiped as the only true God, who was jealous for His name and for the devotion of His people, who punished sin, who loved perfectly, who invoked fear at the slightest glimpse of His glory.

As the Israelites saw the mountain smoking and the lightning, and as they heard the thunder and the trumpet, they physically shook and retreated in fear, widening the distance between God's holiness and their sin. But Moses had a unique relationship with God. He spoke to God personally and visited with Him on the mountain. He was a righteous man, and God's favor seemed to be upon him. So the people asked him to be their mediator, to speak to God on their behalf.

But Moses was a mere man, just like them. He could speak to God on their behalf, but he could not fulfill all the righteous requirements of God's law any more than they could. He could not perfectly obey. He could not bear the weight of their sin. He certainly couldn't die for them. Israel rightly understood their need for a mediator, but what they may not have realized was that they needed a better mediator than Moses.

A better mediator would come, but not in Moses' day. He would come in a time, and place, and under circumstances that no one would expect. Like the Israelites, we also need a mediator, one who would fulfill all the righteous requirements of the law for us (Col. 2:14) and in us (Rom. 8:4), one who would bear the weight and guilt and punishment for our sins, one who would die for us. Scripture tells us that "there is one God, and there is one mediator between God and men, the man Christ Jesus, who gave himself as a ransom for all" (1 Tim. 2:5). Christ fully obeyed all the laws of God. He never failed. And God, in His kindness, did "what the law, weakened by the flesh, could not do. By sending his own Son in the likeness of sinful flesh and for sin, he condemned sin in the flesh, in order that the righteous requirement of the law might be fulfilled in us, who walk not according to the flesh but according to the Spirit" (Rom. 8:3–4).

Write a sentence that communicates what you learn about Christ from Exodus 20.

Close your time today in prayer, delighting in God for sending Christ as our perfect mediator.

DAY FOUR

God's compassionate response to Israel's dreadful fear is a call to worship. The altar would be the *way* that God draws *near*. "In every place where I cause my name to be remembered *I will come to you* and bless you" (Ex. 20:24).

This had to be reassuring to the Israelites, calming their fear of approaching a holy God. The Lord had already said that they should *not* come near to Him (Ex. 19:12). Instead, after Moses had consecrated the people, he brought them to the foot of the mountain and the Lord descended on Mount Sinai. *He* came down to *them* (Ex. 19:11, 18) to bless them by giving them laws to obey in demonstration of their love for Him (Ex. 20:6).

Moses reminds them that God came to test them so that they would not shrink back in trembling fear but would instead worship Him alone and not fall into idolatrous sin. The altar would be a place of atoning for sin, a place where peace with God would come through a blood sacrifice.

In one sense, as we close Exodus 20, we see the trajectory that shows us that God's laws were meant to help Israel have a right relationship with God that would lead them to a right worship of God. The relationship that God called His people to would require the perfect obedience of Christ, the only One who could bridge the immense gap between the holy God and sinful humanity. It is through Christ that we can obtain a relationship with God that allows us to speak to Him personally, and to worship Him in reverent fear.

Christ is the Mediator of a new covenant, one in which the law is written on our hearts and minds, and is founded upon the law of Christ, which commands us to love God and to love one another (Matt. 22:37–40). The promises of the new covenant come to believers through faith in Christ, in order that He might redeem us from sin, secure our eternal inheritance, and purify us for good works. We contribute nothing to the saving work of Christ in our lives. It is all God's work. We only respond to it by turning away from our sins and turning to Jesus for a covenant relationship with God.

What has God done to initiate our relationship with Him?

John 3:16

Romans 6:23

Hebrews 10:17–18

1 John 4:9–10

How does the Bible teach us to respond to God?

Romans 10:9–10

Romans 12:1–2

Hebrews 4:16

Hebrews 12:28

What does your relationship with Christ look like on a day-to-day basis?

Is there anything you would like to change about your relationship with Christ?

Are you drawing near to Christ, or shrinking back from Him in fear of condemnation?

How can you tune your heart to obedience and service out of love for Christ?

What are some ways in which you can show the love of Christ to those in your:

family/home

work or school

church community

neighborhood

other

Answer for today, this week, this month, and this year.

Draw near to Jesus, responding to His love for you by loving others.

DAY FIVE

CONTRIBUTION TO THE LAW

In Exodus 20, our Sovereign God calls Israel to a covenant relationship with Himself and their neighbors through the Ten Commandments, so that they might live in proper fear and worship of Him. As we explore the themes of God's relationship with His people and their response to Him throughout the book of Exodus, we get a clearer picture of how this book contributes to the genre of the law.

READ EXODUS 6:2–8.

How did God initiate a personal relationship with His people?

READ EXODUS 34:6–7.

What do you learn about the character of God?

READ EXODUS 34:27–28.

What do you learn about God's relationship to Israel?

READ EXODUS 4:30–31; 14:30–31; 19:8.

What are some positive ways that God's people responded to what they saw and heard from the Lord?

READ EXODUS 15:24; 16:2–3, 8; 32:7–9.

What are some negative ways that God's people responded to what they saw and heard from the Lord?

Based on all you have read in this lesson, how would you describe what God intended when He established His covenant with Israel?

How do these verses help you understand God's intentions for us as we read the Pentateuch?

Literarily, Exodus starts off as an action-packed epic drama, where the main character, Moses, comes on the scene, immediately drawing you into his story and into the story of the suffering of the nation of Israel. The drama continues through chapter 19 and shifts from narrative to speeches and legal codes for the remainder of the book.

The legal codes begin with the moral laws that include the Ten Commandments. It goes on to outline various civil laws governing how the people live in a covenant community. And finally covers ceremonial laws regarding the construction of the tabernacle with all its utensils and furnishings and the priests' attire that would all be used for the worship of God. These instructions were given by God through Moses to Israel, for the purpose of God establishing His covenant with Israel so that He would dwell with them as their God.

We would do well to delight in and worship God for revealing Himself to us and calling us into covenant relationship with Him through Christ. Next week, we will learn how God consecrates His people to be set apart as holy.

QUESTIONS FOR GROUP REFLECTION

1. How does the commandment to love God and love your neighbor summarize the essence of the new covenant relationship with God?

2. Reflect on a time when you experienced the transformative power of Christ's obedience to the law in your own life. How did this impact how you viewed your circumstance?

3. Consider practical ways in which we can cultivate a deeper reverence for God and a more vibrant worship in our daily lives as a response to Christ's mediation of the new covenant.

4. How does the new covenant relationship with God through Christ empower believers to live lives characterized by love, grace, and forgiveness toward others?

Consecration

(LEVITICUS 20)

For it is the blood that makes atonement
by the life. —Leviticus 17:11

*C*an you relate to this rather humorous quote?

> If you read people passages from the divine books that are good and
> clear, they will hear them with great joy. . . . But provide someone a
> reading from Leviticus, and at once the listener will gag and push it
> away as if it were some bizarre food. He came, after all, to learn how to
> honor God, to take in the teachings that concern justice and piety. But
> instead he is now hearing about the ritual of burnt sacrifices![3]

This is the perspective of many as they wade through the book of Leviticus. Pages
and pages of animals killed, dismembered, and burned. Their blood sprinkled all
over the place, and much of it around meals and festivals. Add to that, there are
loads of strange laws such as those that forbid cutting of beards, tattoos, eating
shellfish, and wearing clothes with mixed fabrics. They leave us scratching our
heads trying to determine how any of this applies to us today.

And on top of all that, this week you get to read one of the most difficult chapters
in all of Leviticus. It is a chapter that centers around child sacrifice and sexual
immorality. It is dark and difficult and will likely still leave you with many
questions. But stay with it. I hope that this chapter will also illuminate Christ in
beautiful ways and help you to see the unique contribution that Leviticus makes to
our understanding of the law.

DAY ONE

CONTEXT OF THE PASSAGE

Israel is still camped at Mount Sinai, three months after God delivered them from Egypt (Ex. 19:1–6).

God gives Israel the Ten Commandments. He then begins to show them what proper fear and worship of God looks like in verses 18–26. Specifically, in verses 22–26, the Lord tells Israel to build an altar where they would offer sacrifices to the Lord. The altar would be the place of blessing for Israel as they remember the name of the Lord and as He meets with them. Also, in Exodus 20:18, the Lord descended on the mountain as a display of His glory. After the book of the covenant was read to the people, God directed Israel to contribute to the building of a sanctuary so that He would dwell with His people (Ex. 25:8–9).

Once this sanctuary was complete with all the furnishings, altar, and the ark of the covenant, as well as the priests' garments, the glory of the Lord filled the tabernacle (Ex. 40:34–35). Thus, the place of worship was established. Now the people of worship needed instructions on how and why they were to worship God.

Chapter 20 of Leviticus contains mostly rules and regulations that provide warnings against spiritual and sexual unfaithfulness. Undergirding these warnings is the reminder that God calls His people to be consecrated as holy unto Him, because He is holy. This chapter echoes many of the rules and regulations from Leviticus 18, but with the added consequences for disobedience.

Exodus is the story of *what* God expects of His people. Leviticus is the story of *how* the Lord intends for them to carry out His expectations. The book of Leviticus opens with the Lord showing them what it looks like to wholly devote themselves to God. In order for Israel to live as God's *holy people*, they had to offer a *holy sacrifice*, one that was without blemish, one that was pleasing to the Lord.

These sacrifices had to be offered by a *holy priest*, one who was consecrated, set apart by God to offer the sacrifice on behalf of the people and to make atonement for their sins. It was the job of the priests to "distinguish between the holy and common, and between the unclean and clean, and . . . teach the people of Israel all the statutes that the LORD has spoken to them" (Lev. 10:10–11). The holy priests made these offerings in a *Holy Place* (Lev. 16), the altar that is in the tabernacle of the Lord. The people would bring their sacrifices to the entrance of the tent of meeting (Lev. 6:16, 30).

Once a year, on the Day of Atonement, Aaron would go into the Holy Place that is "inside the veil, before the mercy seat that is on the ark" (Lev. 16:2). If Aaron went at any other time, and in a way that God did not prescribe, he would die. It was at this time that Aaron would make a sin offering for himself, for all the other priests, for the people, and for the Holy Place "because of their transgressions, all their sins" (Lev. 16:16). The climax of this annual ritual was for Aaron to confess all the sins of the people on the head of a live goat. The goat would not be killed, but would be sent into the wilderness, *bearing the iniquities of the people on itself* (Lev. 16:20–22). Imagine. The weight of all the sins of all the people would be placed on the live goat, and the goat would be relegated to live out its existence in the wilderness away from the presence of God and the people of God and the place of God. The people's sins would be forgiven and cleansed and cast outside of the camp.

READ LEVITICUS 20.

What stands out to you as you read? You may want to circle or underline words and phrases that are repeated and highlight what seems significant to you.

What aspects of God's character do you see most clearly in this passage?

Chapters 18 and 19 establish the immediate context of Leviticus 20. Read the following passages from those chapters and answer the questions:

What additional information do you find in Leviticus 18:1–5 that is not included in Leviticus 20?

Skim Leviticus 19, with particular attention to the last phrase in each paragraph. What is repeated? What do you think it communicated to Israel? How would this affect how they understand Leviticus 20?

How does this reflection affect how you understand Leviticus 20?

DAY TWO

COMMAND OF THE TEXT

Leviticus 20 actually takes us back to Leviticus 18, where much of what we see in chapter 20 is echoed, but without the accompanying consequences.

Chapter 18 is full of prohibitions, all of which deal with sexual sins that are practiced in Egypt and in Canaan (Lev. 18:3), which result in both the people and the land being unclean (Lev. 18:24–25), and the consequences are summarized as "the persons who do them shall be cut off from among their people" (Lev. 18:29). Instead, they are to obey the Lord because, as He states, "I am the LORD (your God)" (Lev. 18:2, 4–6, 21, 30). Obedience leads to life—"if a person does them, he shall live by them" (Lev. 18:5).

In the law books, we want to first look for instructions, commands, or laws. What is God asking of His people, or what direct commands is God giving? Why does He issue those commands? What does He want His people to know, believe, and do?

READ LEVITICUS 20:1–2A AND 18:21.

Who are the speakers and audiences?

What is God forbidding? How does God view this practice? What is the punishment?

What is God forbidding? How does God view this practice? What is the punishment?

How are these verses different from 20:1–6? What two things does God command? What is the basis for these commands?

READ LEVITICUS 20:9–21. For these verses, list what God is forbidding and the punishment for engaging in the forbidden practice, and where the accountability lies.

v. 9:

v. 10:

vv. 11–12:

v. 13:

v. 14:

v. 15:

v. 16:

v. 17:

v. 18:

v. 19:

v. 20:

v. 21:

In these verses, who is accountable for his or her actions?

What are some commonalities that you see from these verses with regard to the sinful practices, punishments, and consequences? Read Leviticus 20:22–24a. You might also want to compare Leviticus 18:3–4, 24–30.

What does God positively command in v. 22 and what would be the result?

In v. 23, what happens to the nations that practiced wicked customs?

According to v. 24, what is God's promise and the blessing that comes as a result?

According to Leviticus 20:24b–26, how does God identify Himself? What has He done for Israel and why?

READ LEVITICUS 20:27.

What is God forbidding in this verse, and what is the punishment? (A necromancer is one who contacts or conjures up spirits of the dead.) How does this differ from v. 6?

Let's take a closer look at a few themes from this chapter. **What categories of sin does God warn Israel against?**

What is the difference between a punishment and a consequence, in the way that we see them in this chapter?

What does God warn would happen to people who commit these sins?

What does God assert about Himself?

What does God require from His people?

How would the people meet God's requirements?

Putting it all together, write a sentence that communicates what Leviticus 20 would have meant to the Israelites.

Sin is serious and will be judged by God because He is holy and has called us to be distinct from the people around us. Idolatry will not be tolerated. Sexual immorality will not be tolerated. God ultimately enacts judgment for sin even when He uses human agents to carry out His judgment.

The consequences of sin are serious. Whether the sin is individual or communal, private or public, religious, intellectual, or social, God will punish all sin. He ain't playing with us. That's why He says over and over again, "consecrate yourselves." It's the holy version of "check yourself before you wreck yourself." Separate yourself from the godless people around you and devote yourself fully to the Lord. In essence, "Be holy, for I am the LORD your God . . . I am the LORD who sanctifies you."

DAY THREE

CLUES ABOUT CHRIST

At the outset, this seems like a very strange chapter to use as an illustration of how the book of Leviticus fits into our understanding of God's law. However, this chapter specifically emphasizes several themes that we find throughout not only Leviticus, but the entire Bible, that anticipate our Lord and Savior Jesus Christ. Jesus likely used the book of Leviticus to teach that all of Scripture is about Him (Luke 24:27). Let's consider the themes of holiness, cleansing, and atonement from Leviticus 20 that relate to what Jesus has done for believers.

HOLINESS

"They shall be cut off" (Lev. 20:3, 5–6, 17–18)

READ NUMBERS 6:22–26.

How does God bless His people?

SEE EXODUS 19:4–6.

Based on these verses, why would it be so bad for God to set His face against His people?

READ GENESIS 17:14.

What does being cut off from the community indicate regarding one's relationship with God?

SEE MATTHEW 27:46.

What do Jesus' final words before His death indicate about His relationship to the Father at that moment?

READ ROMANS 9:2–3.

What would Paul give in order to see his kinsmen according to flesh come to saving faith in Christ?

READ 1 PETER 2:9–10.

What does Peter call believers in Christ?

Cleansing

"Their blood is upon them" (Lev. 20:9, 11, 13, 16)

READ GENESIS 9:6.

What was the consequence of shedding human blood?

In 2 Samuel 1, an Amalekite man confesses to killing King Saul, saying Saul begged the man to finish him off, since he was about to die as a result of battle (vv. 6–10).

What was David's response to the Amalekite for killing King Saul according to vv. 14–16?

What does "your blood be on your head" indicate about the person who sins?

READ 1 JOHN 1:7.

How does the blood of Jesus differ?

Describe the significance of Pilate's statement in v. 24 and the crowd's statement in v. 25.

Although we are at fault for our sins, what does Jesus' shed blood mean for us according to Isaiah 53:4–5, Ephesians 1:7, and Revelation 5:9?

ATONEMENT

"They shall bear their iniquity" (Lev. 20:19)

READ ISAIAH 53:6, 11–12.

What do these verses say about the Messiah to come?

According to John 1:29, who is Jesus and what does He do?

READ 2 CORINTHIANS 5:21, HEBREWS 9:28, AND 1 PETER 2:24.

What do these passages say about Jesus? About believers?

Atonement means to make amends for a wrong, to relieve God's anger caused by our sin. In the Old Testament, atonement comes from the word that refers to the mercy seat. This was the covering on the ark of the covenant, on which blood was sprinkled by the priest on the Day of Atonement, to make atonement for, or cover, the people's sins. God would frequently appear in a cloud above the mercy seat to speak to His servant Moses and the people of Israel, giving them commandments and instructions that He expected them to obey.

The repeated phrases of "cutting off," "blood being upon them," and "bearing iniquity" clearly teach us that sin has consequences for the individual or community who commits them—guilt, death through the shedding of blood, and separation from God and from people. Because they are no longer a part of God's covenant community, they cannot experience the blessings that God promised to them.

The person whose blood is upon them bears the responsibility for their sin. It is their own fault, and they must be held accountable. The one who bears their iniquities carries the full weight of their sin, and it remains with them. The good news of the gospel is that Jesus died for all of our sins. Jesus' *blood* was shed in the place of ours. Jesus took our *sins (iniquities)* upon Himself. Jesus was *cut off* from God on the cross so that we would not have to be cut off from Him eternally. All of this was so that we would be the holy people that God called us to be, that we might die to sin and live righteously before God, eagerly waiting to receive our eternal inheritance.

Write a sentence that communicates what you learn about Christ from Leviticus 20.

Close your time today in prayer, delighting in God that through Christ we can be the holy people of God.

DAY FOUR

HOLINESS

Not separated *from* but separated *to* the Lord; Jesus was cut off so that we could draw near.

Spiritual Implications

The law warns us against idolatry. Idolatry includes both false worship and false wisdom. In Leviticus 20, the warning is against idolatry that puts the lives of children at risk, and idolatry that turns to sorcery and the occult. Sacrificing children to a false god was horrific, one of the practices of the pagan peoples around them that God warned the Israelites to stay away from. It may seem like a distant concept to us today, but we need to understand the culture. "Images of [the idol] Molech were made of bronze, and their outstretched arms were heated red-hot. Living children were then placed into the idol's hands and died there or were rolled into a fire pit below. Some sources indicate a child might also be 'passed through the fire' prior to the actual sacrifice in order to purify or baptize the child."[4] That was the appalling, idolatrous practice that God sternly warned His people against.

Today when we think of idolatry, we often refer to more subtle ways of engaging in false worship, such as the worship of wealth, possessions, and people. False wisdom comes in many forms, including practicing witchcraft and sorcery, but also valuing any worldly wisdom above God's wisdom that is found in the Bible. Warnings against all forms of idolatry were meant to teach God's people to consecrate themselves, to set themselves apart, so that they would be distinct from the nations and people around them who did not know or love God.

How can you live differently from the world by fleeing idolatry?

How can you actively engage in efforts to protect the lives of children, physically and spiritually? Be as specific as you can in your answers.

Relational Implications

The law warns us against relational sin. The Bible condemns sin against children, parents, all manner of sexual sin, whether in or outside the institution of marriage, irrespective of consent. Human bodies are sacred and meant to be holy to the Lord. As image bearers, the dignity of people is displayed in honoring one another. Dishonoring bodies demonstrates that one's heart is aligned with worldly, pagan practices.

Sex is an intimate privilege reserved for a husband and wife to honor God and one another in their union. Any sexual practice or thoughts outside of that context dishonors God and those who are made in His image. Sexual sins, including adultery, incest, and homosexuality, are all condemned throughout the Bible. Jesus condemns sexual immorality from the moment of thought, not just action (Matt. 5:27–28; Mark 7:2–23). Yet, the gospel of Jesus also holds out grace for those who flee sexual sin and repent (1 Cor. 6:18–20).

How can you honor God and those made in His image by fleeing from relational sin?

Who can you turn to for accountability to guard against sexual sins?

God called His people to consecrate themselves, while also affirming that He is the One who is consecrating them, setting them apart so "that you should be mine" (Lev. 20:26). God's promises are not dependent on our faithfulness. He remains gracious and kind to us, even when we fall short.

We have the same calling as ancient Israel, to be wholly consecrated to and for God. And what He calls us to, He also provides. God's promises are rooted in His Son, as the Word reminds us that all of God's promises are fulfilled in Christ (2 Cor. 1:19–20). The law points forward to the only One who could perfectly obey the Father, our Lord Jesus Christ. He became obedient to the point of death on a cross. It is only the cleansing blood of Jesus that atones for our sins and makes us God's holy people.

In what ways have you dishonored others in your thoughts or actions? Repent and receive Christ's forgiveness.

CLEANSING

The law makes it very clear that the one who sins bears the responsibility for their own sins. We learned that the consequence of shedding human blood is for the guilty person to be put to death. In this sense, the shedding of blood brings about condemnation. It proves our guilt. However, the good news of the gospel is that Jesus was the One punished for our sins. Jesus' blood does not bring condemnation, His blood cleanses. His blood redeems. His blood offers forgiveness and reconciles us to our holy God. There is no other way for humanity to be reconciled to God, except through the blood of Jesus. What cleanses us from our sin, and restores us to God, and purifies us from unrighteousness? Only the blood of Jesus.

What blessings might you experience from receiving Christ's cleansing?

ATONEMENT

The law teaches us that not only must we accept responsibility for our sins, but we must be ready to accept the consequences as well. This is what it means to "bear our iniquity." It carries with it the idea of a burdensome weight, such as in Leviticus 16:22 when the scapegoat was sent into the wilderness bearing all the iniquities of the people on itself. God instructed Ezekiel to take upon himself the sins of Israel and Judah, to suffer because of their sins, not his own (Ezek. 4:4–6), illustrating the truth with an object lesson. What a picture of Jesus, who took our sins upon Himself, bearing the weight of our sins to the point of death in order to make atonement for us, covering us with His righteousness so that we could be reconciled to God.

As we close out today, ask God to show you what might be making you hesitant to accept responsibility for your sins.

DAY FIVE

CONTRIBUTION TO THE LAW

The book of Leviticus teaches the Israelites, and shows us, the requirements of holy living. It requires sacrifice, cleansing, atonement, and holiness. God's holy people were meant to be in community with each other and the Lord. The sacrificial system was how God would cause His people to live distinct from the nations around them. God showed them how seriously He takes sin, how devoted He was to their purity (cleanliness). The consequences of sin are severe, but the benefits of obedience to God's law are stunningly beautiful.

Literarily, Leviticus is utopian literature, which means it shows us what the ideal society looks like, including the people and structures that produce and sustain it. For the believer, the ideal society is one that reflects God's holiness, and in the book of Leviticus, the structures that produce this ideal society are the sacrificial system, the priesthood, and the many rules and regulations *for* cleanliness and *against* idolatry. These structures were meant to guide God's people living together in community and were meant to show those outside the community that Israel was different and separate, consecrated to God. Their distinctiveness would be a witness to the world around them.

The book of Leviticus teaches us that consecration requires both killing sin in all its forms and knowing the blessings of Christ's obedience and sacrifice which allows for the righteous requirements of the law to be fulfilled in believers who walk according to the Spirit in love for God and our neighbors.

Read through these passages from Leviticus: 5:14–16; 6:14–18, 25–27; 7:1; 10:3; 11:44–45; 20:26; 21:7–8.

How is the theme of holiness developed in Leviticus through these verses?

CLEANSING AND ATONEMENT

Read through these passages from Leviticus: 1:3–5; 3:1–2; 4:3–7, 27–30; 5:9–10; 10:10–11; 11:47; 13:45–46; 15:31.

How do the themes regarding what is clean and unclean relate to atonement?

God made the Sabbath day holy (Gen. 2:3). He called the ground on which Moses stood holy (Ex. 3:2). God made the priestly garments holy (Ex. 28:2). God made the food, the altar, the tabernacle, the tent of meeting, the priestly crown, the furnishings—all of it—holy. He made Israel a holy nation (Ex. 19:4), and then in Leviticus 11:44–45, God sets the people of Israel apart, individually and collectively, as holy. Not only that, but the Bible repeatedly says that whatever touches the holy things also becomes holy (Ex. 30:25–27; Lev. 6:14–27).

This is why God admonishes Israel to not to be like the people of Canaan when they enter the land, and not to do like the Egyptians whose land they just left. He reminds them of who they are and whose they are. "You shall be holy to me, for I the LORD am holy and have separated you from the peoples, that you should be mine" (Lev. 20:26).

Holiness is such a foundational concept for the Christian life yet is beyond human capacity to fully understand or to live out. We are called to be something that we are incapable of by our own efforts. We are tempted to want God to tell us to *do* holy things, things that we can see, handle, touch. We think that by doing holy things, it makes us holy people. But God didn't say, "Do holy." He said, "Be holy."

He called light and sky and water and plants into existence by proclaiming, "Let there *be* . . ." In His sovereign power, He caused things that did not exist to take on form and function. The act of *being* precedes *doing*. If we think that our standing as God's holy people is primarily an act rather than a state of being, then we make ourselves legalists and distanced from the grace of the gospel. If we focus on *being* God's people by living our lives for the glory of Christ, then He will enable us by His Spirit to do those things that are in accord with holiness.

Delight in our God who has consecrated us, set us apart as holy. Next week, we will learn how His people dove into chaos, the consequences that resulted, and the gospel response to their, and our, rebellion.

QUESTIONS FOR GROUP REFLECTION

1. Consider the contrast between the deadly consequences of sin and the life-giving promise of holiness through Christ. How does this contrast shape our understanding of God's grace and redemption?

2. Consider the role of the Holy Spirit in sanctifying believers and conforming them to the image of Christ. How does the Holy Spirit empower us to live holy lives despite the presence of sin in the world?

3. Reflect on the relationship between forgiveness and holiness. How does God's forgiveness of our sins through Christ motivate us to pursue holiness?

4. Discuss the importance of community and accountability in the pursuit of holiness. How can we support and encourage one another in our journey toward holiness?

Chaos

(NUMBERS 14)

Then the LORD said, "I have pardoned, according to your word.
But truly, as I live, and as all the earth shall be filled
with the glory of the LORD . . ." —Numbers 14:20–21

*I*t's pretty customary for children to become impatient on long car rides and flights. The infamous "Are we there yet?" question seems to come pre-wired in the minds of children who find it difficult to sit in one spot for more than a few minutes, or who are so excited for the adventure ahead that time seems to stand still.

My son was born on a small Caribbean island with a total landmass of 102 square miles. The entire country is about one and a half times the size of Washington, DC! What we considered a long car trip was the thirty minutes it took to drive to our favorite beach. And the timing was so long only because the speed limit for most of the drive was around 30 mph. When we moved to a large city in the United States, we drove forty-five minutes to the children's school, and four to six hours to visit family. Needless to say, after about thirty minutes of driving, the "Are we there yet?" mantra started. We encouraged our son to take a nap to let time fly by, but you can probably guess what his first words were post-nap!

Now imagine you're an ancient Israelite camped at the foot of Mount Sinai for about a year. Just last year, God had rescued you from harsh Egyptian enslavers. You survived plagues, you've been fed daily with manna from heaven. God has been with you, as evidenced by a cloud during the day and a pillar of fire at night. You fought and defeated attackers. God gave you the moral law explaining how to live rightly before Him and before your neighbors. He outlined civil laws to govern the nation. He gave you ceremonial laws pertaining to worship. He gifted you with skill to build the tabernacle, the ark of God, and the tent of meeting with all of the accompanying utensils and furnishings. Yes, you have rebelled against God, but He has consecrated you as His special creation. He is committed to carrying out His covenant to bless you, by bringing you to the land of Canaan that He promised your forefather Abraham.

And now, over four hundred years after the promise to Abram, the answer that generations have been looking forward to is almost realized. To the question "Are we there yet?" the answer is "almost." It's kind of like driving into the parking lot of the amusement park, where you can see the giant roller coasters, hear the delighted screams and laughter of the crowds, even smell the popcorn and funnel cakes. But you still have to park the car, pay for your ticket, and wait in a painfully long line before you enter the park.

The sights, sounds, and smells of the promised land must have been palpable. The priests and heads of tribes were given their job descriptions. Final preparations had been made for consecrating the people. They celebrated the Passover. Israel organized themselves at Sinai by tribal camps according to God's instructions. God had to set them straight because of their complaints about food and leadership. But finally, they arrive in the desert of Paran in the city of Kadesh-barnea (Num. 32:8) about eleven days later. They hung out in the desert for forty days waiting for a report from the twelve scouts who went before them into Canaan to spy out the land (Num. 13:1–20). What was the purpose of spying out the land? It was not meant to elicit fear or doubt in the people. Rather, it was meant to prepare them for what lay ahead, to renew their trust in the Lord, to raise the battle cry and forge ahead in faith.

The spies' report spooked the people because the Canaanites looked invincible (Num. 13:30–33). Though God had delivered them from the hand of Pharaoh, preserved them despite their disobedience, and provided manna for them daily, they still thought it safer to run in fear rather than to walk in faith. They were so close to the land of promise, yet they were so far away from trusting the God of promise.

DAY ONE

CONTEXT OF THE PASSAGE

The historical context of Numbers 14 starts back in chapter 11. Only three days into their journey from Egypt, when the ark of the Lord went before them to find "a resting place for them" (Num. 10:33), the people started complaining "about their misfortunes" (11:1). I mean, could they really be calling God's provision for them over the past year "misfortunes"?

God was not having it, and His anger "was kindled" and the "fire of the LORD burned among them" and some of the outer regions of the camp were consumed. In fear, they cried out to Moses (see Num. 11:1–2), Moses interceded on their behalf, and the Lord stopped the fire. But that didn't really put the fear of God in them, because there was still a group of complainers craving the food that they'd had back in Egypt, and discontent with the daily manna the Lord had been providing (vv. 4–6). God was angry. Moses was done. Moses was not able to bear the burdens of the people alone (v. 15). The Lord commissioned the elders of Israel, seventy men in whom He placed His Spirit, to help Moses lead the obstinate people (vv. 16–17).

Their complaining was ultimately not about food. Rather, they were rejecting God, basically saying that He wasn't enough for them (vv. 20–23). God responded in judgment by giving them more meat than they could handle until they were sick of it. Surprisingly, given all that he had seen God do in the past, Moses responded in disbelief that God could provide food for over six hundred thousand every day for a month (vv. 20–23)! God was like, "Just you wait and see." And just as He said, the Lord did bring an abundance of meat in the form of quail. The people gorged themselves on it, and the Lord sent a plague throughout the community that killed many of them (vv. 31–33).

Not only did *the people* complain about their misfortune, lack of meat, and too much manna, and not only did *Moses* complain about the people's burdens, but now Moses' *siblings* complained about his Cushite wife, which seems to be an ethnic complaint. This was next level complaining, because the Lord called all three of them out to the tent of meeting (12:1–4). It's like your parents discovering their favorite vase is broken, and they call all the kids at once to find out who did it. Whenever parents call all the kids at once, out of the blue, it's usually not a good sign.

It's like God was saying, "All of y'all come here, right now." God made it clear to them that Moses was a special prophet whom He spoke with clearly, face to face (Ex. 33:11). And not only that, but when Moses asked to see the Lord's glory, God graciously responded, "I will make all my goodness pass before you (Ex. 33:19). So now the Lord asks Moses' siblings rhetorically, since they knew the special relationship that He had with Moses, why they were not afraid to speak against Moses (Num. 12:6–9). God "said what He said," and when the cloud of His presence left the tent, Miriam was left with leprosy (12:10). Aaron appealed to Moses and Moses pleaded with God to heal her, but though she would be healed, God's punishment stood and the entire Israelite community had to wait until Miriam's seven-day isolation outside the camp was over before they could continue to Paran (Lev. 13:4).

The complaint intensifies in chapter 13 beyond their misfortunes, to Moses' leadership, to God's provision, to complaining about God's promise to bring them safely into Canaan. Canaan was the place where this nomadic, landless people would finally be able to plant their roots so that they could worship God freely, and so that God would dwell with them in a more present and permanent way than He ever had before.

What stands out to you as you read? I encourage you to circle or underline words and phrases that are repeated and highlight what seems significant to you.

What aspects of God's character do you see most clearly in this passage? Take a moment to thank God for who He is.

DAY TWO

COMMAND OF THE TEXT

In Numbers 13, God sent explorers to scout out Canaan as the people prepared to enter. Moses sent a leader from each of the twelve tribes to report back. Ten of the spies minimized the good of the land, and instead focused on the strength of its inhabitants. Two of the spies, Caleb and Joshua, encouraged the people to go immediately in obedience to God's instructions and occupy the land, emphasizing their trust in the power and promises of God. As you read this chapter, keep in mind that Israel is on the brink of bringing into fruition a promise that their forefathers and God Himself had been reminding them of for centuries!

Where are the Israelites at the opening of this chapter (v. 26)?

Who are the main characters in the chapter? What is driving their responses?

In Numbers 14:4, what do the Israelites conclude in response to the scouts' report as documented in 13:25–33? How does their response differ from Joshua's and Caleb's assessment?

In Numbers 14:11–12, what is God's reaction?

What does Moses ask of the Lord in verse 19, and what is God's answer in verses 20–23?

What happens in verses 28–35 that correspond to verses 2–4?

How do we see God's grace in verses 28–35?

What do verses 2–4, 9, 11, 22, 27, and 44 reveal about the people's character and their view of God?

Based on what you have discovered in this chapter, how does God's plan to give Israel the land of promise keep moving forward?

Putting it all together, write a sentence or two that communicates what this passage would have meant to the Israelites.

God spared Israel from immediate death, demonstrating His forgiveness. He immediately destroys the ten scouts by plague and the nation of Israel must still suffer the consequences of their sins. In dramatic and very specific, climactic fashion, God punishes Israel with what they most feared: death in the wilderness (14:29, 32–33, 35). Their fear kept them from receiving a generations-long promise from God. Maybe this is why the repeated refrain in Joshua is "be strong and very courageous" (Josh. 1:6–7, 9, 18). This would have been a message for Joshua, but also for all the young Israelites who grew up watching their older family members and friends die as a result of their fear and distrust.

Fortunately, this isn't the end of the story, as we'll see tomorrow!

DAY THREE

CLUES ABOUT CHRIST

God would not stand for the grumbling and complaining forever. In fear, when Israel saw God's glory on the mountain after the giving of the Ten Commandments, they begged Moses to speak to God on their behalf (Ex. 20:18), and Moses did just that. When they sinned with the golden calf, Moses interceded for them, and God relented from destroying them (Ex. 32:11–14). And now here, Moses refers back to God's previous acts of mercy toward Israel and appeals to Him to be gracious yet again by pardoning the sins of Israel.

He is a patient and forgiving God, which He had been showing them over and over again (Num. 14:20). The psalmist reminds us that "he said he would destroy them—had not Moses, his chosen one, stood in breach before him, to turn away his wrath from destroying them. Then they despised the pleasant land, having no faith in his promise. They murmured in their tents, and did not obey the voice of the Lord" (Ps. 106:23–25). And God would continue to pardon even in the midst of His judgment by not destroying the entire nation immediately, but by causing them to "bear [their] iniquity forty years" (Num. 14:34) until the entire generation had died out. In this chapter, we see the rebellion of Israel, we see Moses again interceding on behalf of His people, and we see God extend mercy and pardon to Israel, though still judging them for their sin. Let's see how these themes serve as pointers to Christ.

Rebellion and Judgment

According to Isaiah 53:12, how does the Suffering Servant (Christ) identify with Israel? (Note: *transgressors* can be translated as *rebels*.)

What does "yet he bore the sin of many" indicate about the Suffering Servant?

Intercession

In Numbers 14:13–19, what sort of prayer do we see Moses praying (e.g., praise, confession, intercession)?

What does the Suffering Servant do for the transgressors in Isaiah 53:12?

What do Hebrews 7:25 and Romans 8:34 say Jesus is doing now for believers?

According to Romans 8:26–27, who else is interceding for believers?

According to Romans 2:4, what is God's kindness in pardoning (forgiving) meant to produce in His people?

Write a sentence that communicates what you learn about Christ from Numbers 14.

Close your time today in prayer, delighting in God for accepting Christ's perfect sacrifice and receiving Christ's perfect intercession on our behalf.

DAY FOUR

CARRY THE TEXT WITH YOU

Israel's playlist is on repeat. They cycle through periods of disbelief and rebellion. While those tracks are playing, Moses breaks in with commercials by way of intercession where he recounts God's faithfulness to Israel in the past and appeals to God for pardon of their sins. But God owns the streaming service, and none of what they experience is outside of His overarching plan. His plan to bring His people into the land of promise keeps moving forward even with their continued grumbling, complaining, and unbelief. Numbers 14 shows us the devastating effects of rebellion against God, our need for a mediator to intercede on our behalf, and the gracious pardon that God offers in the midst of His righteous judgment of our sins.

Are you knowingly being disobedient in some way in your life? How does your awareness that Jesus allowed Himself to be "numbered with the transgressors" (Isa. 53:12) prod you to confront this area in your life?

Name a situation in your past in which you've witnessed God's faithfulness.

How does the memory of God's faithfulness in the past inform your prayers?

What impact does knowing that you are not alone in coming before God have on you? (Remember Rom. 8:26–27, 34.)

Revisit Numbers 14:20 and Romans 2:4–5. If we know that God's kindness is meant to lead us to repentance, what might He be leading you to repent of right now?

Take a moment now to ask for God's forgiveness, knowing He is faithful and just to pardon our sins and cleanse us from all unrighteousness (1 John 1:9–10).

DAY FIVE

CONTRIBUTION TO THE LAW

The book of Numbers, and chapter 14 in particular, teaches us that God's plans cannot be thwarted. He will do all that He has promised. He will accomplish all that He has set out to accomplish. God expects Israel to occupy the land of promise. Instead, they cower in fear and refuse to enter. Numbers demonstrates God's faithful care of Israel through their wilderness wanderings despite their constant complaining and rebellion.

Literarily, Numbers is primarily narrative with bits of law and poetry mixed in. These narratives (stories) function to highlight what God expects of His people. God expects us to live in loving obedience to His Word; however, our sinful hearts rebel, grumble, and complain. We waver in our faith and find it difficult to trust God at times. But God is faithful and continues to carry out His purposes for us despite our fear and unbelief. Israel's history, including the cycles of rebellion, Moses' intercession, and God's judgment, are referenced over and over throughout the Scriptures.

In Psalm 106, the psalmist recounts the Israelites' experiences in the wilderness. Verses 24–27 summarize Numbers 14 specifically. The rest of the psalm paints a picture of Israel's continued acts of rebellion throughout their wilderness journeys.

READ PSALM 106:43–48.

What were God's actions toward Israel? What was Israel's response? What did Israel finally do that caused God to look upon their distress? (vv. 43–44)

What did God remember, what did God do, and why? (v. 45)

In vv. 47–48, what reason do the Israelites give for crying out in repentance?

How does this tie into what we learned about God in Weeks 3–4 of this study?

How does this contribute to your understanding of what the Law is all about?

On the surface our lives may seem to wander from one place to the next, driven off course by our grumbling and sin. Yet under and through and behind it all, there is a guiding hand, a divine Author, penning the entire grand narrative, scripting it to the conclusion He Himself has written for us. There is a bigger storyline to our personal stories, an intricate plot that will, after all of life's twists and turns, end with Him bringing us into the place He has prepared for us. That is the reality to which we need to firmly hold. That is what it means to live by faith: to affirm the reality of God's hand over our lives even when we cannot see it with our eyes.[5]

God's law is very relevant for us today. There is much that we can learn from the Israelites. Scripture reminds us that what happened to the nation of Israel serves as examples for us so that we would not sin as they did by testing God, grumbling, falling into idolatry, and practicing sexual immorality, among other things. These things "were written down for our instruction" (1 Cor. 10:1–13), to warn us against evil and to direct us toward Christ.

Often people like to talk about their own "wilderness experience," drawing parallels from Israel's experience. While we might suffer hardship that we need to persevere through, it would be good for us to remember that Israel's wilderness experience was a direct result of their sin. It was not the case that they were in the wilderness because they had stumbled on hard times. No. Their wilderness wandering was what happens when God's merciful pardon is met not with repentance and revival but with continued rebellion.[6]

The good news that should guide us is that despite our continued rebellion, Jesus' plan of redemption, of taking us to our eternal inheritance, of bringing us home to glory, continues to move forward. Next week, we will learn how God continues to call His people to covenant commitment to Him.

QUESTIONS FOR GROUP REFLECTION

1. Reflect on the ways in which Jesus' plan for redemption unfolds despite human disobedience throughout history. How does this give us hope in the face of our own failures and shortcomings?

2. Reflect on a time when you witnessed Jesus' plan moving forward despite human rebellion, either in your own life or in the lives of others. How did this experience shape your understanding of God's sovereignty?

3. Discuss the role of faithfulness and obedience in aligning ourselves with God's plan. How does our response to God's leading impact the fulfillment of His purposes?

4. Reflect on the relationship between human agency and divine providence. How do we reconcile our responsibility to make choices with God's sovereignty over all things?

Commitment

(DEUTERONOMY 30)

And the LORD your God will circumcise your heart
and the heart of your offspring, so that you will love the
LORD your God with all your heart and with all
your soul, that you may live. —Deuteronomy 30:6

*B*efore to any Disney vacation with young children, parents often hype up all the cool stuff children will experience, like the big castle, the awesome rides, the yummy food, meeting their favorite characters, and the epic fireworks show. But what we often fail to tell them is that the walking will get old sooner than they think, the long lines will test the patience of the entire family, we will not allow them endless amounts of cotton candy and ice cream, and oversized mascot characters can be a bit scary.

We forget that when the oldest sibling faced the massive Sir Topham Hat character at the train museum, she freaked out and ran away from him. Yeah, that might happen at Disney too. Children will likely get dirty and grumpy and complain . . . a lot. And by the time the fireworks show starts late in the evening, they may be too exhausted to enjoy it. Never mind that the screamers and firecrackers may be too loud for little ears. But we want them to be pumped about their adventure, so we hope that all the fun stuff will outweigh our growing worries or potential hiccups. And if families happen to make more than one trip to Disney, parents learn to prepare children in advance so they might have the best experience and loads of fun.

Just as parents prepare their children for Disney World with the hope of creating a positive and exciting experience, in the closing chapters of Deuteronomy we see God directing Israel's final preparations before entering the promised land, and we sense their excitement mixed with a bit of trepidation. In Deuteronomy 30, God challenges Israel to make choices that will lead to a fulfilling and blessed life in Canaan.

DAY ONE

CONTEXT OF THE PASSAGE

After God's judgment that Israel would wander in the desert forty years for their disobedience and disbelief, He continued to provide laws and instructions to Israel that they would need in order to govern themselves not only in the wilderness, but also when they would finally get to Canaan, the land of promise. During these years, Israel encountered conflicts with neighboring nations, and the cycle of Israel's sin, God's judgment, His mercy, and their fickle recommitments continued to define their relationship with the Lord.

As the book of Deuteronomy opens, Moses delivered a series of speeches and instructions to the Israelites, covering various aspects of governance, morality, and the covenant between God and Israel. Through Moses' recap of Israel's history and exhortations to live in accordance with God's Word, God continues to remind Israel of His expectations for them in this covenant. He wants their wholehearted devotion.

In chapters 1–3, Moses takes Israel *back* in history, from where their parents first received God's commands at Mount Horeb, recalling God's faithfulness to them in the midst of their rebellious ways.

In chapters 4–26, Moses exhorts Israel to face the *present* by acknowledging their wavering commitment to the Lord and calls them to faith and obedience "with all their hearts and all their souls." It's a heartfelt and personal plea for them to follow

God's law from a heart that really believes in Him and trust that His commands are right and good. Chapters 27–29 focus on the covenant between God and Israel, the blessings and curses associated with obedience and disobedience, and the importance of upholding God's covenant from generation to generation.

READ DEUTERONOMY 30.

What stands out to you as you read? You may want to circle or underline words and phrases that are repeated and highlight what seems significant to you.

What aspects of God's character do you see most clearly in this passage?

READ DEUTERONOMY 28:1–2, 9–10.

What would be the result for Israel's obedience?

What would be the consequence for Israel's disobedience according to 28:36–37 and 63–64?

READ DEUTERONOMY 29:3-4.

In all that the Lord had done for Israel, what had they yet to experience from God?

READ DEUTERONOMY 29:9-15.

What is God's desire for Israel? (There's a lot here.)

What does this communicate about God's desire for you?

DAY TWO

COMMAND OF THE TEXT

The second generation of Israelites are in Moab at the border of Canaan, knowing that once they enter the land, Moses and the Levites will divide Israel between two mountains—Mount Gerizim to receive God's declaration of blessing for Israel's obedience, and Mount Ebal to receive God's declaration of curses for Israel's disobedience (Deut. 11:29). That must have been quite a scene! Then, in Deuteronomy 28:36, Israel is told very clearly that they will eventually choose a king for themselves, fall into idolatry, and go into exile. Yet, God also affirms in 29:10–15 that He will still uphold His end of the covenant He established with them by leading them into the land of promise, establishing them as His people, and dwelling with them as their God.

He restates the terms of His covenant in detail in chapters 27–29. He promises abundant blessings to Israel if they carefully obey His commands, and grave curses upon them if they disobey. God's affirmation of His commitment to Israel extends not only to them but also to future generations if they faithfully "do all the words of this law" (Deut. 29:29). As we study Deuteronomy 30 today, keep in mind the question, "What does God want them to understand about His law and their ability to fully obey?"

In verses 1–2, by "these things," Moses is looking ahead to the time when Israel would experience the curses for falling into disobedience. What should Israel then do and with what posture?

According to verses 3–6 and 9, how will God respond to His people as a whole? Regarding their hearts? Regarding their fortunes?

What will God do to their enemies (v. 7)?

In verse 8, what does God expect from Israel in return?

What is God's posture toward Israel and what is this contingent upon, according to verses 9–10?

READ DEUTERONOMY 30:11–18.

From verses 11–14: What does God say about the choice before them (v. 11)? What do the questions in verses 12–13 indicate about God's commands? In verse 14, what is God leading Israel to understand about His Word?

From verses 15–18: What are the two options before them? How would an Israelite show he or she has made the better choice, with what result?

.

If the other choice is made, what would be the result (vv. 17–18)?

READ DEUTERONOMY 30:19–20.

What does God tell the Israelites to do and why? What does that look like?

The phrase "the LORD your God" is used more than fifteen times in this chapter. What does this communicate about the relationship between God and Israel?

What would you say God was ultimately calling Israel to through their obedience?

Putting it all together, write a sentence or two that communicates what this passage would have meant to the Israelites.

This chapter serves as a bookmark that Israel can come back to when the blessings and curses actually occur. God says "when" all these things happen, not "if." It's like a paper clip in the book of their lives that they can come back to when they "come to [their] senses" (Deut. 30:1 CSB[7]). Israel is reminded of what God's Word is, where God's Word is, and how to embody it. The Word of God is the Word of Life that they must continually choose to obey, every day, with every decision, in the midst of temptation and idolatry and all manner of sin. God's commands are not too hard for them nor too far from them, because the Word is embodied *in them*. The next lesson will help us to see exactly how this is true.

DAY THREE

CLUES ABOUT CHRIST

The contrasts between obedience and life and blessing versus disobedience, death, and curses cannot be missed in Deuteronomy 30. The rhetorical questions from verses 11–14 indicate God knows that what He is calling them to do could feel like a weight that is too heavy for them to carry. God states what He knows is in their hearts. "God, this is too hard. It's an unattainable goal. We can't do it." In a way, they're right—in an ultimate sense, they cannot fully obey. They know that they need an intermediary, and even seem to know that the intermediary could not be Moses, hence the questions "Who will ascend . . . who will go . . ." Let's explore the answers to these rhetorical questions and how they anticipate our Lord and Savior Jesus Christ.

READ JEREMIAH 31:31–33.

In the new covenant, where will the law reside? How will this affect the relationship between God and His people?

According to Exodus 19:7–8 and 24:3, what have Israel's past responses to God's commands been?

Based on Deuteronomy 30:11, although no response from Israel is recorded, what does this verse imply?

READ DEUTERONOMY 30:12–14 AND ROMANS 10:5–10.

What empowers obedience to God—both for Israel and for us?

REVISIT DEUTERONOMY 30:15–20. READ JOHN 1:1–4 AND 14:6.

Where is true life found?

It had to be mind-boggling for Israel to hear that God's commands were not just on tablets of stone, but that they embodied the Law (the Word is *in them*). God gave them the gift of faith, placing His Word *in their hearts* so that they would believe and placing His Word *in their mouths* so that they would confess that He is Lord.

The Word, who was in the beginning with God and was indeed God, who has life in Himself and who gives life and light to all who believe in Him, is Jesus. Jesus is the Word who became flesh and dwelt among us as Immanuel, God with us. In Him resides life, light, grace, and truth. God's commands are impossible for us to perfectly obey, but they are possible for Jesus, and He proved it by perfectly obeying the law in our place. And though He obeyed all of the law of God fully, He still suffered and died on the cross as penalty for our sins. His death brought salvation and eternal life to all who have faith in Him. Jesus is the way to God, the truth of God, and the perfect embodiment of life in God.[8]

Write a sentence that communicates what you learn about Christ from Deuteronomy 30.

Close your time today in prayer, delighting in God that through Christ's perfect obedience to the law, we can live a life of faith and obedience to God.

DAY FOUR

The heart of humanity is often geared toward something other than the simplicity of obedience. Not that it's easy to obey, but God says over and over again in His Word to obey Him, to do what He's asked us to do. And He's given us the ability to do it. That ability comes from faith in Christ.

What makes obedience simple is faith. Trusting the Lord gives us Spirit-empowered ability and courage and joy to walk in obedience to Christ. Someone has said "our native tongue is Law." People like rules, but rules devoid of relationship can feel punitive rather than protective. God's commands are not meant to trip us up or to keep us in fear and doubt. No. His Word is a lamp for our feet and light for our path (Ps. 119:105). His commands revive our souls, make us wise, give us cause for rejoicing, and enlighten us. His law is true, pure, righteous, and sweet (Ps. 19:7–10). His testimonies are our delight and joy (Ps. 119:14, 111). His Word is a person, Jesus Christ, who gives us life and breath and everything. Therefore, in faith we choose to live a life that is pleasing to Him.

How would you describe your current relationship with Christ?

Does it seem that God's commands are too hard for you or too far off? Why or why not?

Which commands do you find most difficult to obey and why?

What motivates you to choose life and good (obedience)?

What tempts you to choose death and evil (disobedience)?

How does Jesus' perfect obedience challenge or encourage you?

What daily practices demonstrate that you are living a life of faith in Christ?

How might your recognition that this life is preparation for an eternity with Christ affect your daily choices and priorities?

The Israelites were already the people of God, yet He still called them to choose life; the same is true for us. Our union with Christ doesn't eliminate persistent choice in the mundane, everyday habits of life. We are empowered to choose Christ because we have the spirit of God living in us. Obedience outside Christ won't work; it will be shortsighted, and we will fall to the ways of the world. The bottom line: continually choose life in Christ. When you sin and realize it, repent and turn to God in obedience. We can do this because the Word is in us. We can do this because our hearts and souls are turned toward the Lord in love.

DAY FIVE

CONTRIBUTION TO THE LAW

The book of Deuteronomy is an emotionally moving book, an impassioned plea for God's people to renew their covenant commitment to Him by choosing a life of obedience to God. It teaches us that our obedience to God's law comes from faith, trusting the Lord with all our hearts and souls. It teaches us that His commands are not empty words for us. They are our life (Deut. 32:47).

Throughout the Pentateuch, God directs Israel to obey from the heart. He warns that idolatry will draw their hearts away from Him. The book of the law—the Pentateuch as a genre—will be a witness against Israel because they are rebellious and stubborn people who will eventually turn away from the law of God. God sends Moses to die on Mount Nebo, where he could see the land of Canaan that he would not enter because of his own sin. In effect, the law would not save him, Israel, or us.

Yet, God promises that one day He will make a new covenant with Israel. This new covenant will not be on tablets of stone as it was with Moses, but it will be written on the hearts of God's people (Jer. 31:33). Christ is the Mediator of this new covenant (Heb. 9:15), which is universal in nature, including both Jews and Gentiles (Gal. 3:14). Sacrifices, rituals, and offerings are no longer necessary because the new covenant promises the complete and eternal forgiveness of sins through the sacrifice of Christ once for all time (Heb. 10:12, 18). Finally, and most importantly, the new covenant is an eternal, everlasting covenant (Heb. 13:20) bought with the blood of Christ that secures a permanent relationship with God, not based on mere obedience to the law but rooted in the obedience that comes from faith in Christ.

FAITH AND LIFE

READ DEUTERONOMY 4:1; 5:32–33; 8:1; AND 11:8–9.

What is the relationship between obedience and life?

READ PSALM 106:23–25 AND HEBREWS 3:16–19.

In these passages, disobedience is equated to what?

What is the relationship between belief and salvation?

God does not sugarcoat the reality of the challenges the Israelites will face from the nations around them. He very clearly warns them about how their hearts will be tempted to turn away from Him. He front-loads the scary stuff, the limitations He places upon them for their good and His glory. He reminds them of how their parents had failed by despising His Word, complaining, and fearing man more than they feared Him. He specifies how He intends to bless them when they commit their lives to Him in obedience, and the dire consequences should they choose to disobey. So that He is crystal clear, He lets them know that the choice before them should be a no-brainer—so choose life! And they *say* that they will do all that the Lord commands, but their hearts are not fully committed. Their subsequent history would play this out. The Scripture teaches that our salvation involves both confession with the mouth—"I will do all that the Lord says" (Ex. 19:8)—and belief in the heart—"I delight to do your will, O my God" (Ps. 40:8).

God does not sugarcoat what the Christian life will be like either. Jesus tells us that we will experience trouble in this world (John 16:33). His Word also reminds us that the enemy prowls around like a lion seeking someone to devour (1 Peter 5:8). But Jesus has overcome the world, so we can resist the devil. The Lord has given us everything we need for life and godliness in this fallen world (John 16:33; 1 Peter 5:8; 2 Peter 1:3). These truths allow us to acknowledge both the harsh and thrilling realities of life, and to persevere in them so that we might experience one of the greatest blessings that comes from a life of obedience and faith, and that is God's delight in us (Deut. 30:9).

To choose life is to commit ourselves daily to Christ, meditating on His Word day and night, delighting in the law of the Lord, for in His commands is where we find delight. Take a few moments to meditate on Psalms 1:2 and 119:35.

QUESTIONS FOR GROUP REFLECTION

1. Consider the implications of God giving Himself to His people. How does this relational aspect of God's character impact our understanding of His love and grace and our response to Him?

2. Reflect on the role of the Holy Spirit in enabling us to live lives of faith and godliness. How does the indwelling presence of the Holy Spirit empower us to live according to God's will and purposes?

3. Reflect on a time when you experienced the difference between outward religious observance and genuine heart devotion. How did this experience shape your understanding of God and yourself?

4. Discuss practical ways in which we can deepen our faith in Christ and continually choose a life of faithfulness. How can we support one another in this journey?

Christ in the Law

The law was our guardian until Christ came,
in order that we might be justified by faith. —Galatians 3:24

I was born on the cusp of the popularization of color TV. For most of my early childhood, black and white shows were the norm. One of my family's favorite TV programs was *The Andy Griffith Show*. The show centered around Andy Taylor, a young sheriff in a small country town, much like the small town I was raised in. He was a single father to his son Opie, and a man who liked to do things by the book. He was a walking diary of southern idioms, colloquialisms, and proverbs. Opie figured out life as he lived it and kept Sheriff Taylor on his toes as a parent. As an elementary-aged boy living in a small community, he roamed around town fishing, riding his bike, and spending time with his friends.

In one episode, Opie met a hobo named David Browne. David hopped trains and stole food and was not having the best influence on Opie. Sheriff Taylor decided to talk to David, to encourage him to be a better role model for Opie. When Sheriff Taylor challenged him about his lifestyle, David said, "I'm not above bending the law now and then to keep clothes on my back or food in my stomach."

Andy responded, "You can't let a young'un decide for himself. He'll grab at the first flashy thing with shiny ribbons on it, then when he finds out there's a hook in it, it's too late. The wrong ideas come packaged with so much glitter it's hard to convince him that other things might be better in the long run, and all a parent can do is say, 'Wait. Trust me,' and try to keep temptation away."[9]

Some of us are like David. We're probably not hobos, but maybe we have a hobo mentality. We think the law is bendable, especially if it suits what we think we need and what we want. In our society, and throughout time, people have often seen the law as man-made restrictions that we adapt to our circumstances. But what if we're wrong about what we think we need? What if we're wrong about the way we go about meeting our needs?

Andy is right. Left to ourselves, we reach for what looks good, and when we find out that everything that glitters isn't gold, it may just be too late. In the law, God knows what His people need. He knows what is best for them. And He provides as a good father would. He guides them and teaches them what is best for them, but His people are too easily lured by the flashy things with shiny ribbons, and the Lord has to continually call His people back, saying, "Wait. Trust Me."

God has made promises to His people that *will* come to pass, and that *have* come to pass. From the beginning, the Lord gave commands to His people, that through their obedience, He would bless them and their descendants, and all the nations of the earth. His commands are grounded in His promises, enacted because of sin, and they bear witness about Christ. This week, we will study how the New Testament church grappled with these issues of obedience to the law and faith in Christ.

DAY ONE

CONTEXT OF THE PASSAGE

This entire study has been an exploration of the Law so that we might see its relevance for today. The questions around the promises of God, obedience to the law, and faith are ancient. Just like Israel and the early church, believers today desire to obey the Lord. We desire to grow in our faith, and we feel the tension of wanting to "do" the right thing when it comes to our faith.

The book of Galatians gives us a sneak peek into some of these tensions in the early Christian church, particularly the tension between the law and faith in Christ. The main disagreement concerned Gentile converts to Christianity, whether they needed to observe the law and if men needed to also be circumcised to be considered true Christians. A Jewish sect called Judaizers maintained that Gentile believers must adhere to Jewish customs, which caused confusion and division in the church.

In Galatians 2:11–21, we learn about a related situation involving Peter, an apostle of Christ who became a leader in the early church. Peter believed Gentile believers should be accepted into the Christian community, but his own actions proved inconsistent. When he was with his Jewish friends, he followed dietary rules and imposed these on Gentiles as well. But, when he was with Gentiles, he ate like Gentiles and did not adhere to dietary rules. This inconsistency created confusion in the church.

This passage teaches us about the dangers of legalism[10] and the importance of relying on faith in Christ, not on mere obedience to the law for justification.[11] Peter's actions remind us that it's not following the law, but only faith in Christ, that makes us right with God. This was true for Israel, for the early church, and for us today. Israel trusted in the Promised One to come. We trust in the Promised One who was revealed to us in the person of Christ.

In Galatians 3, Paul details the relationship between faith, the law, and the promises of God. He brings heavy theology to the level of the ordinary people who wanted to understand how to live out the gospel in their daily lives. He emphasizes that faith does not stand in opposition to the law and God's promises. Rather faith is the connective tissue that binds the law and the promise of God.

READ GALATIANS 3.

What stands out to you as you read? You may want to circle or underline words and phrases that are repeated and highlight what seems significant to you.

What aspects of God's character do you see most clearly in this chapter?

What words are repeated in these verses? What is the main idea indicated in these verses? How do these verses add to your insight from Galatians 3?

As you close your time in today's study, meditate on what it means to you to be Abraham's offspring (Gal. 3:29).

DAY TWO

COMMAND OF THE TEXT

Galatians 3 brings us face to face with questions about the interplay between faith, the law, and God's promise to Abraham. If it's a promise, then why do we need to obey? If we can only receive God's blessings through obedience, but we know we cannot be perfectly obedient, then are we doomed? And where does faith come in? These are all valid questions that Paul addresses to a church that is being influenced by a group called the Judaizers who were trying to convince them that the only way to be righteous before God was through obedience to Jewish traditions and law, such as requiring circumcision before one could become a Christian. Paul exposes the true intent of the Judaizers as both pride and fear. They wanted to avoid persecution for teaching the cross of Christ by outward shows of obedience meant to impress others (Gal. 6:12–14).

Paul zooms back and tries to lay some theological foundations upon which the church should place their understanding of the interplay between law and faith. He calls the church back to the basis of their own salvation and takes them to the law itself and to the example of Abraham who first received God's promise to show how God's plans and purposes have not changed. He explains the Old Testament teachings about righteousness, faith, the law, the gospel, the promises of God, as well as our union with Christ and with other believers, whether Jewish or Gentile.

READ GALATIANS 3:1.

How does Paul describe the state of the Galatian church? What have they seemingly forgotten?

According to verses 2 and 14, what is the connection between the Spirit and faith?

In verse 3, what is the connection between faith and the beginning and ending of our spiritual lives?

How is God's role described in verses 4–5?

What do Genesis 15:6 and Galatians 3:6 say about Abraham?

According to Galatians 3:7, what does it mean to be a son of Abraham?

How was the gospel preached to Abraham and how do believers receive this blessing from Abraham?

For some additional background, read Deuteronomy 27:26, Habakkuk 2:4, and Leviticus 18:5.

Now see Galatians 3:10–14 to answer the following:

What is the result for those who rely on the works of the law?

Verses 11 and 12 might sound like contrasting ideas. What does each verse say about how a person receives life?

How does verse 13 resolve these contrasting ideas?

What is the blessing of Abraham in verse 14, and how does one receive the Spirit?

What is the blessing that God promised to Abraham in Genesis 12:7 and 22:17?

READ GALATIANS 3:15–22.

According to verses 19–20, why was the law given? How does the law relate to the promise given to Abraham?

READ GALATIANS 3:23–29.

What were believers like under the law according to verses 23 and 24?

What are believers like under Christ according to verses 25–29?

Putting it all together, write a sentence that communicates what this passage would have meant to the early church.

In the midst of the Judaizers' confusing, divisive teaching that one must basically convert to Judaism and adhere to Jewish traditions and laws in order to become a true Christian, Galatians 3 reminds the church that God justifies believers by faith in Christ and gives us His Spirit by faith, so that we might be free *from* the law and free *to* live as God's diverse people united by that same faith. Take a moment to thank God for this freeing truth.

DAY THREE

CLUES ABOUT CHRIST

I've never met anyone who has forgotten their own testimony. Everyone I've met can tell their story of what their lives were like before they met Jesus, what blinders existed that kept them separated from Christ, and the circumstances that led to their understanding the gospel and placing their faith in Jesus alone for salvation. Their personal testimony of the work of Jesus in their lives demonstrates that their spiritual eyes have been opened to the truth.

Such was the case with those in the Galatian church, but now they are acting as though circumcision and following Jewish customs and laws are necessary for them to be true followers of Christ. Paul says that the Galatian church has been bewitched! It is as if someone has cast a spell on them and caused them to forget their own testimony, what they have seen with their own spiritual eyes and what they have heard with faith (Gal. 3:1–2). Paul's concern is that they are turning away from Christ and turning to a different gospel, a gospel that is really no gospel at all.

The word gospel literally means "good news," but a gospel forged by man is not good news; it is deadly because it is a gospel that cannot offer eternal life. Only the gospel of Jesus Christ can do that (Gal. 1:6–12). Paul makes it clear that it is actually foolish to have the Holy Spirit residing in them by faith but allowing themselves to be led by their flesh (Gal. 3:3).

He goes on to explain that the true children of Abraham are those who believe the gospel just as Abraham did, not those who obey the law because no one can perfectly obey the law (Gal. 3:7–14). The Israelites began to understand this (see Deut. 30:11–14) and Paul wants the Galatians to do the same. This passage illustrates Jesus' relation to God's promise to Israel through Abraham, the law, and the primacy of faith. He wants them to see that faith in Christ, not works of the law, frees and unites all believers, whether Jewish or Gentile.

Let's unpack these a bit more to better understand the unique ways in which this passage connects the law to Jesus and the church.

FORGIVENESS

READ ACTS 13:37–39.

Who can receive forgiveness of sins, and how?

The righteousness of God is referenced in our next passage. A good description of His righteousness is "God's moral virtue and excellence that prompts Him to do all that He does, including bringing people into a proper relationship with Him, but also judging people for their sin."[12]

READ ROMANS 3:22–31.

How is God's righteousness made known to us?

What is true of all of humanity that warrants our need for justification?

How is one justified by God?

Why can we not boast in our works?

Respond to these questions, prompted by the verse(s) referenced.

What has Jesus freed us from (Rom. 6:22)?

What has Jesus freed us to (1 Peter 2:16; Gal. 5:13–14)?

What does slavery to sin look like (Gal. 5:1–4)?

In contrast, what does slavery to Christ look like (Rom. 6:18)?

What is our relationship to the law now (Rom. 7:6–7; 8:1–2)?

UNITY

According to John 1:12, Romans 8:14, and Galatians 3:27, who can be included as children of God?

How does our union with Christ impact:

The promise made to Abraham (Gal. 3:14; Eph. 3:6; Heb. 9:15)

Our relationship to the law (Gal. 3:13; 5:18; Matt. 5:17; Rom. 13:8)

Our relationships with the Father and the Son (Gal. 4:4–7; Rom. 8:16–17)

Our relationships with other Christians (Eph. 2:16; Col. 1:20–22; 2 Cor. 5:18)

Our witness to the world (John 13:34–35)

Anyone who places their faith in Christ receives forgiveness of sins and obtains right standing with God. Our righteousness is not based on the law. If it were, we would have to obey the law perfectly. We know this is impossible. This is what Paul means by "the curse of the law" (Gal. 3:13). But because of Jesus' perfect life of obedience to the Father, His death as the sacrificial Lamb who takes away the sins of the world, and His victory over death and the grave means anyone who trusts in Him can be justified before God and receive His righteousness.

As those who are justified freely by God's grace, we are free from the law and free to serve the living God, loving and serving God and one another. This is actually how the law is fulfilled—by love, not by legalistic obedience. Does this mean that we don't have to obey the law? No, it means that Jesus obeyed the law perfectly in our place. It means that obedience is not a burden for us, but the Spirit enables us to obey God's commands as an expression of love for Christ.

It is no light matter that anyone who calls on the name of the Lord shall be saved. Our salvation has personal, global, and cosmic implications. Personally, we are saved from the wrath of God because of our sins, and we are reconciled to God, no longer enslaved to sin but servants of our holy and perfect Master who does all things well. Our salvation serves as a witness to a watching world, making our love for one another attractive to those who do not yet know the love of God through Christ. When God saves us, we are born, as God's adopted children, into a living hope through the resurrection of Jesus Christ, to an imperishable, undefiled, and unfading inheritance that is kept in heaven for us until our salvation is complete at the end of time (1 Peter 1:3–5). We are fellow heirs with Christ, sharing in His sufferings, resurrection, and the glories of the kingdom to come.

Write a sentence that communicates what you learn about Christ from Galatians 3.

Close your time today in prayer, thanking God for freeing us from the law through faith in Christ.

DAY FOUR

CARRY THE TEXT WITH YOU

FORGIVENESS

Faith and forgiveness are intertwined. Faith is not a performance-based system, at least not our performance. God's forgiveness is not based on anything that we do. We cannot earn our way to God. Faith is the result of Jesus' performance. His real-life actions on our behalf were not a show but a sacrifice, demonstrating God's power and love to all who believe in His Son. There is no forgiveness for anyone who does not place their faith in Christ.

Consider the message of the gospel and the offer of forgiveness and eternal life through faith in Christ. What does this mean to you?

How can you rest in God's grace rather than striving to earn salvation or favor with God through your works?

In what areas of your life do you struggle to believe God's promises to love you, forgive you, guide you, and give you eternal life in Christ? What might you ask of the Lord to help you live in light of these promises?

FREEDOM

Freedom is a scary word! We can be paralyzed by it or abuse it. We love it but often don't know what to do with it when we have it.

What a beautiful gift that Christ has redeemed us from the curse of the law, offering us freedom from the power of sin, guilt, and condemnation. Our acceptance before God is secure in Christ so we do not have to fear freedom. Crossing the boundary lines of freedom should be so distasteful and unappealing to us that we are not tempted to breach its borders where the prowler waits to devour us.

Where I grew up it was not unusual to see cows grazing in a pasture as we drove on long stretches of country roads. Every pasture was bounded by some sort of fence. Interestingly, the fencing never seemed strong enough to keep a 1,500-pound animal from breaking loose. I always found it interesting that no matter how shabby or flimsy the fence that bordered the pasture, the cows never seemed to try and break free. They seemed peaceful and content to graze within the boundaries set for them.

Upon closer inspection, I realized that many of these fences contained barbed wiring or thorns. I'm sure it would only take one attempt to dissuade the animal from getting too close. The boundaries set for them not only encouraged them to stay within the pasture of safety where abundance and provision resided, but also protected them from predators that might jeopardize their safety. Either way, there was freedom inside the fence and risk outside it.

The pasture of freedom is so vast that we can explore within its borders, under the care of our Good Shepherd, grazing daily on its bounty without fear.

What areas of your life tempt you to test the borders of your freedom in Christ? How might you avoid those temptations?

In what areas of your life do you experience and enjoy the freedom that Christ offers? How can you use your freedom to better serve God and your neighbors?

UNITY

Because faith in Christ transcends every worldly distinction, unity should mark the Christian community across every ethnic, cultural, social, and economic difference. Our diversity should beautify the gospel of Christ and the Christian church, not be the cause of divisiveness and dissension. We are united to Christ and to one another as children of God, fellow heirs with Christ, and witnesses to a watching world.

Are there factors that make this kind of unity difficult for you? Why do you think that is?

How can you cultivate unity and reconciliation:

In your personal relationships

In your local church

In your community

Pause and ask God to help you proactively seek unity in any areas lacking in your own life.

DAY FIVE

CONTRIBUTION TO THE LAW

Galatians is a letter within the epistles genre written to teach the church how to live under God's law. Specifically, this book teaches believers how to live in the freedom and power of the Holy Spirit through the gospel of grace, which offers forgiveness through faith in Jesus Christ. Like all of the epistles, Galatians includes doctrinal teaching, correction, guidance for Christian living, pastoral care, and application to the unique needs and challenges of the church.

It is essential to understand Galatians for its unique contributions in instructing and nurturing the faith and practice of the church as it relates to the connections between the law, faith, freedom, and the promises of God. We have seen these connections in several places throughout the Scriptures and explored their implications for understanding core principles of the Christian faith. Those core principles emphasize justification by faith, freedom from legalism, the continuity of God's plan, unity in Christ, and the practical application of these truths in the lives of believers.

Galatians offers a rich theological framework for Christian living and relationships within the church. We understand that forgiveness can be found in no other name than Christ. We understand that Christ offers not only forgiveness, but freedom from sin and freedom to obey and love God with all our hearts, minds, and souls.

An encomium is a special type of writing that praises a character, concept, or quality.[13] It follows a standard pattern that typifies this kind of writing. The elements of an encomium introduce the concept being praised, reveal the origins of the concept, list the unique distinctions or qualities of the concept, and demonstrate the supremacy of the concept. It also provides a concluding exhortation to the readers to follow in like manner, praising the concept. We see that pattern in Hebrews 11.

Let's end this week meditating on this beautiful chapter and give God praise for the beautiful continuity of His Word from the law to the letters. Please turn to Hebrews 11.

What is the concept that the author is praising or elevating (v. 1)?

What is the origin of this concept (v. 2)?

In the lives of the Old Testament patriarchs and heroes, what are a few distinguishing attributes of this concept (vv. 3–40)? You may want to choose two or three individuals from this passage to highlight.

How are we exhorted to imitate these saints of old (Heb. 12:1–3)?

How is this concept seen as supreme over other things (Heb. 11:4, 13–16, 26, 40)?

What is the most supreme example that believers should imitate (Heb. 12:2)?

From beginning to end, the actions and character of biblical heroes and villains are meant to stir in Israel, and in us, hearts of obedience to the Lord that stem from faith in God's promises that still stand to this day.

- God's promise of an offspring that would come from Abraham and through whom all the nations would be blessed finds its fulfillment in Christ.

- God's promise that blood makes atonement for sin finds its completion in Christ.

- God's promise to pass over those covered in the blood extends to all who trust in Christ.

- God's promise of pardon to Israel for all their sins comes through Christ.

- Every offering and sacrifice and Levitical priest are but shadows and examples that point us to Christ.

- God's promise to circumcise the hearts of His people comes through the circumcision of Christ.

Indeed, every promise of God finds its *Yes* in Him (2 Cor. 1:20). For from Him and through Him and to Him are all things. To Him be glory forever. Amen (Rom. 11:36).

QUESTIONS FOR GROUP REFLECTION

1. Reflect on the concept of justification by faith in Christ. How does this understanding shape our perspective on salvation and our relationship with God?

2. Discuss the hope of an eternal inheritance that is promised to believers in Christ. How does this hope shape our perspective on life and eternity?

3. Discuss the idea of freedom from legalism that comes through faith in Christ. How does this freedom empower us to live lives that are guided by grace rather than by a list of rules?

4. How does faith in Christ break down barriers and bring believers together despite differences in background, culture, or opinion?

CONCLUSION

Remember those so-called daunting books of Leviticus and Numbers? You may have started this study with a bit of trepidation, considering the abundance of rules and regulations stretching before us like an imposing mountain range in books such as these. But now, as we conclude, you have not walked an easy trail, but have traversed the peaks and valleys of these books, discovering the timeless truths they hold for us today.

I hope this study has shown you that God's commands are not a mere collection of arbitrary rules, but a beautiful tapestry woven by God for you. God's commands as given in the law, the Pentateuch, serves as the foundation upon which the entire story of redemption unfolds. From here we see how God's people continued to respond to God's law, and how God has been faithful to His people, revealing His character, pointing to Christ, and providing a canopy of grace for living righteously and joyfully under His commands.

Our journey began with the wonder of creation in Genesis, a reflection of God's power and work and promise of blessing. Exodus unveiled the beauty of the covenant, an unbreakable bond between God and His people. Leviticus exposed the necessity of consecration, a call to live a life of holiness, set apart for God's purposes. In Numbers, we grappled with the chaos of disobedience and its consequences. Deuteronomy reiterated the importance of commitment, a call to choose God's way and reap the blessings He promises.

In each of these books, we found a piece of the grand narrative of redemption. From creation to covenant, consecration to chaos, and commitment, the law has been a guiding light, pointing us toward the ultimate fulfillment of God's law in Jesus. He is the embodiment of God's law, the One who perfectly obeyed it, and the means through which we find consecration and freedom from sin's chaos. He calls us to commit our lives to Him, trusting in His work to redeem us from sin and our lawless thoughts and actions.

I pray that this study has served to help you delight in God's law by understanding how each chapter provides a window through which to see the overall message of each book of the Pentateuch and provides insight into how each book contributes to the law as a whole. The Bible is one grand story, and the law kicks off the story by setting the stage for all that will follow in the rest of Scripture.

We have learned that God made us to have a special relationship with Him through His covenant, where we consecrate our lives to Him in holiness. Even when we allow the chaos of our own hearts and of the fallen world around us to take us off track, God persistently urges us with compassion and patience to commit our lives to Him so we can enjoy the blessing of having Him dwell with us as our God.

Remember that Old Testament commands are not relics of a bygone era. They are living words that continue to speak to us, guide us, and reveal God's purposes. May this study embolden you to walk through the Pentateuch with a fresh perspective, and in so doing find that the law is not a set of chains that bind, but a road map that leads you to a deeper, more intimate relationship with the One who gave it. As you navigate the complex terrain of the law, may you delight in discovering how these ancient commands still matter in our lives today.

[Abraham] believed the LORD, and he counted it to him as righteousness.
GENESIS 15:6

And when I see the blood, I will pass over you, and no plague will befall you to destroy you, when I strike the land of Egypt.
EXODUS 12:13

For it is the blood that makes atonement by the life.
LEVITICUS 17:11

Then the LORD said, "I have pardoned, according to your word. But truly, as I live, and as all the earth shall be filled with the glory of the LORD . . ."
NUMBERS 14:20–21

*And the L*ORD *your God will circumcise your heart and the heart*
*of your offspring, so that you will love the L*ORD *your God with all your heart*
and with all your soul, that you may live.

DEUTERONOMY 30:6

The law was our guardian until Christ came, in order that
we might be justified by faith.

GALATIANS 3:24

Christ is the end of the law for righteousness to everyone who believes.

ROMANS 10:4

OUTLINE OF THE BOOKS OF THE LAW

I pray that *Delighting in God's Law* has whet your appetite to continue feasting on the Word of God. You may use this outline and "A Snapshot of Each Week" on page 11, to guide you in further study of the law.

CREATION	
GENESIS 1–11	PATRIARCHS
GENESIS 12–50	POSTERITY

COVENANT	
EXODUS 1–2	REMEMBER
EXODUS 3–19	RESCUE
EXODUS 20–40	RENEWAL

CONSECRATION	
LEVITICUS 1–15	OFFERINGS
LEVITICUS 16–17	ATONEMENT
LEVITICUS 18–27	HOLINESS

CHAOS	
NUMBERS 1–10	CONSECRATION
NUMBERS 11–25	COMPLAINT/CHAOS
NUMBERS 26–36	COMMUNITY

COMMITMENT	
DEUTERONOMY 1–3	HISTORY
DEUTERONOMY 4–11	HEART
DEUTERONOMY 12–26	HOLINESS
DEUTERONOMY 27–34	HANDOVER

ACKNOWLEDGMENTS

I am profoundly grateful to all those who supported and encouraged me throughout the journey of writing this study.

My prayer team is amazing! Thank you Joani, Kanika, Mandy, Moira, Nadia, Nicole W., Tina.

I'm humbled by the expertise and guidance of wise women such as Ruth, Visha, and Zoe who read portions of the manuscript, providing invaluable feedback. Your insights and perspectives have enriched this project beyond measure. Thank you so much.

I extend heartfelt thanks to Esi and Ashley who co-worked with me, patiently listening and serving as a sounding board as I processed ideas and concepts. Your patience and support have been invaluable.

A special acknowledgment goes to all my friends, colleagues, and mentors who have supported me on this journey; I am deeply grateful. Your belief in me and your unwavering encouragement have made this endeavor possible. Thank you for being a part of this journey.

I must also express thanks to my Moody team, specifically to Judy Dunagan and Pam Pugh. Your patience and wisdom have been such a gift to me.

Saving the best for last, I owe a huge debt of gratitude to my loving husband, Thabiti, and children, Titus, Eden, and Afiya. You are always unwavering with your support, understanding, and patience. Your belief in me and your constant encouragement have been my bedrock in this season. I am deeply grateful for your sacrifices and the countless ways you have lifted me up throughout this process.

To God be the glory.

"I delight to do your will, O my God; your law is within my heart." Psalm 40:8

NOTES

1. You will benefit from reading my book *Literarily: How Understanding Bible Genres Transforms Bible Study* (Chicago: Moody Publishers, 2022).

2. "Understanding the Bible: The Pentateuch," Discovery Series, https://discoveryseries. org/courses/understanding-the-bible-the-pentateuch/lessons/how-does-the-torah-point-to-jesus/.

3. "Origin," as quoted in Joel N. Lohr, "The Book of Leviticus," in *A Theological Introduction to the Pentateuch: Interpreting the Torah as Christian Scripture*, ed. Richard S. Briggs (Grand Rapids, MI: Baker Academic, 2012), 83.

4. "What Does the Bible Say about Child Sacrifice?," GotQuestions.org, https://www. gotquestions.org/child-sacrifice.html.

5. Iain M. Duguid and R. Kent Hughes, *Numbers: God's Presence in the Wilderness*, Preaching the Word (Wheaton, IL: Crossway, 2006), 20.

6. See Ligon Duncan's sermon "Rebellion and Rebuke," preached on August 8, 2007. It can be found at https://ligonduncan.com/rebellion-and-rebuke-623/.

7. This verse is taken from the Christian Standard Bible®, Copyright © 2017 by Holman Bible Publishers.

8. See John 1:1, 4; Matthew 1:36; John 14:6.

9. "Opie's Hobo Friend," *The Andy Griffith Show*, created by Sheldon Leonard, season 2, episode 6, Danny Thomas Enterprises, 1961.

10. Legalism is a term that refers to relying on one's good works to earn or merit salvation. It is what Paul means when he talks about "justification by works of the law" in Galatians 2:15, for example.

11. Justification means how one is made righteous before God.

12. Michael G. Vanlaningham, "Romans," in *The Moody Bible Commentary*, eds. Michael Rydelnik and Michael Vanlaningham (Chicago: Moody Publishers, 2014), 1745.

13. I used Dr. Leland Ryken's definition and elements of encomium as a guide for these questions. They are taken from the *ESV Literary Study Bible* (Wheaton, IL: Crossway, 2019), 1978–79.